Ex Libris

Hugh & Georgie O'Shaughnessy

Sea Combat off the Falklands

Antony Preston

Sea Combat off the Falklands

WILLOW BOOKS
Collins
St James's Place, London
1982

A GRUB STREET BOOK
published by Willow Books
William Collins Sons & Co Ltd
London Glasgow Sydney Auckland
Toronto Johannesburg

First published 1982
© Grub Street 1982

Preston, Antony
Sea Combat off the Falklands
1. Falkland Islands conflict, 1982—Naval operations
I. Title
997'.11   F3031

ISBN 00 218046 4

Filmset in Bembo
by AMR Photosetting, Morden, Surrey
Printed and bound in Great Britain by
Wm Collins Sons & Co Ltd, Glasgow

Contents

Introduction

his book had its origins in the first shocked days after the loss of HMS *Sheffield*, when people who had never expected to see a naval battle in their lifetime suddenly found that the Falklands Crisis was no longer a mere show of force.

For myself, having spent a quarter of a century thinking and writing about naval affairs, it came as a particularly unpleasant mental jolt, to think that ships and men that I had known and written about were burning and sinking 8000 miles away. It was the intention at first to restrict the book to the life and death of the *Sheffield*, but as the news from the Falklands kept coming in it had to be expanded to cover the whole of the campaign at sea.

The book deliberately and especially analyzes the naval and air battles as these have been the most controversial. Because of this the narrative hardly deals with events on land, except where they fit into the scope of the argument; the landings themselves, however, are covered in detail.

Although some of the conclusions will be construed as criticism of official decisions and policies, at no time has it been the intention to cause any anguish to those friends and relatives of the dead, nor to imply any disrespect for the bravery and devotion of those who survived. As one who stayed behind, I can only repeat the admiration which I feel for the men of the Task Force, fighting a brave and determined enemy who was armed with a full inventory of modern, precision-guided and fearfully destructive weapons. They went into battle not knowing what it could be like, and they acquitted themselves honourably.

When acknowledging sources I can only refer readers to the published comments of the BBC and ITN reporters about the difficulties of reporting this war. Whether one was on board HMS *Hermes* or reading the runes of the day-to-day official communiques read out in the Press Centre in Whitehall, the fog of war was never more apparent. Modern high-speed communications made it almost impossible to stop bad news from leaking out, but looking back at the daily reports and comparing them with information now available it is clear that deliberate gaps were left, partly to mislead the enemy but partly to permit 'good news' to be released when it suited Whitehall, and equally 'bad news' was held up until the 'Powers that Be' hoped that it had lost its sting. It should also be borne in mind that some official information will never come out.

Much of the information which has gone into this account, therefore, cannot be attributed, and I would only thank the highly reliable anonymous sources who helped to fill in the gaps in the official narrative and unearth surprising and vital bits of information, and to those correspondents in the Falklands whose pooled despatches and vivid word-pictures helped all of us back home to understand something of what was going on.

My special thanks go to my colleague Michael Gething for describing the air war so much more competently than I could, to Michael Lennon for his excellent photographs (even the ones which did not get into the book played their part in confirming what equipment had been fitted to specific ships), to Robert Ho of the Naval Hospital at Gibraltar for his photographs of ships at Gibraltar and to British Aerospace and Westland Helicopters for permission to use photographs and drawings. I am also indebted to Graham Milloy, Brian Hanrahan and John Jockel of BBC TV News who were more than co-operative in providing photographs.

A special word of thanks must be reserved for John A Roberts, whose excellent line drawings will, I hope, make technical details in the text easier to understand; the Ministry of Defence and Thames Television's 'TV Eye' programme for their help in preparing the *Sheffield* cutaway; and British Aerospace for the Sea Harrier cutaway.

To those friends and colleagues with whom I spent many hours discussing the events in the Falklands I apologize if I have inadvertently plagiarized some of their arguments. Opinions and errors, however, remain my sole responsibility.

Antony Preston London 1982

Chapter 1
The Changing Navy

I t is often asked if surface warships have any role in naval warfare today. Why not build submarines and aircraft, and nothing else? These are legitimate questions for the layman to ask, but they ignore one fundamental truth, that navies do not exist merely to fight, but also to exercise control over the sea.

For Britain, an island nation, that control has always been needed to permit movement of goods and raw materials, the imports and exports which enable her to survive. Equally, the United States as the guarantor of European security needs to be able to resupply and reinforce Europe, and any of her other allies around the world. The strategists like to call it 'power-projection', but it is what our forefathers called 'control of the sea'.

Aircraft can fly across the oceans of the world in a fraction of the time that the fastest ship takes, but the movement of large quantities of material cannot be achieved by airlift alone. During the 1973 Arab-Israeli war the entire fleet of American C-5 Galaxy transport aircraft was needed to supply no more than 50 tanks to the Israelis, whereas one merchant ship carried all the replacement ammunition.

Air power is vital to allow ships to exercise control of the sea, as the recent fighting in the Falklands has shown, and no naval commander would ever contemplate extended operations without air support, but the fact remains that heavy goods and equipment have to be brought in by ships, and that means that they must be protected from all forms of attack.

The submarine is also a very potent warship, particularly the nuclear hunter-killer boat, capable of running for days on end at speeds up to 28 knots (31.8 mph), without coming to the surface. But she has great difficulty in communicating with the surface, and cannot coordinate her movements freely with other submarines or surface ships. She can run at periscope depth and transmit or receive radio messages, but all the time she is transmitting she is giving away her position, and so can only transmit at pre-arranged times of the day. All this makes the submarine a poor escort, although she has a role to play in conjunction with other types of warship.

In short, naval warfare is a complex and interdependent business, and the choice of what ships to build has been bedevilled by the rapid advances in military technology which have taken place in recent years. Not only have weapons become more destructive but also more accurate, and so the countermeasures to defend against them have become ever more complex and costly.

The cost of a medium-range anti-aircraft missile system on a ship (the word 'system' is current today to cover the components, such as the launcher, loading gear, tracker radars and the extensive computers and displays) can easily exceed £30 million, and each round may cost £100 000 or more. The ship itself is comparatively cheap to build, for the hull accounts for less than 10 per cent of the cost.

Since the Second World War the Royal Navy has based its main offensive strength on naval aircraft, while devoting its main defensive effort to anti-submarine warfare. After the Second World War the aircraft carrier was recognized to be the most potent form of warship, and until 1966 this view was virtually unchallenged. The Korean War, the Suez Crisis in 1956 and the Indonesian Confrontation in 1964 all proved the utility of the carrier, with its ability to provide the Fleet with defensive air cover and to strike at targets many miles away.

Then in 1966 came a shattering blow, when the then Secretary of State, Denis Healey announced that the Royal Navy would not be allowed to replace its ageing carriers in the mid-1970s. A projected design, designated *CVA-01* was cancelled, and the Navy was told that its air-defence would henceforward be provided by shore-based RAF Phantoms. The only air support directly provided by the Navy would be in the form of helicopters, some operating from frigates and destroyers and others from shore stations. The thinking was logical; the British were withdrawing from 'East of Suez' and their role as a 'world policeman'. The only role, it was argued, should be the defence of North-western Europe within the NATO Alliance, where ships would always have protection from shore-based aircraft, both patrol and interceptor.

This decision proved unworkable, not through any lack of effort by the RAF and the Navy to achieve success, but because the RAF was already overstretched in meeting its other commitments and because the nature of naval operations dictates a much more rapid response than any shore-based aircraft can provide.

The Soviet threat

All the while the Soviet submarine threat was increasing, with new and more potent designs coming forward. The Royal Navy's main role has long been to defend the Eastern Atlantic under the overall command of NATO's Supreme Allied Commander, Atlantic (SACLANT), and for many years British ships have totalled 70 per cent of the so-called CINCEASTLANT command.

It was realized belatedly that the RAF could not provide adequate air cover for the Fleet, and it was decided to equip the three *Invincible* class ships with the Sea Harrier FRS.1. A simple invention, the 'ski-jump' extended the Sea Harrier's range and payload, and was fitted to the *Hermes* as well.

The only effective way of preventing these submarines from breaking out into the Atlantic to attack shipments of troops and material to Europe is seen to be the blocking of the so-called GIUK Gap, the passage between Greenland, Iceland and the United Kingdom; if the Russians can be penned behind that comparatively narrow passage then the vital NATO supply-lines across the Atlantic can be defended.

The main offensive task of locating and bringing to battle the Soviet Northern Fleet is entrusted to the US Navy's Carrier Battle Groups, but the equally important defensive task of escorting and supporting operations in the Eastern Atlantic and the GIUK Gap is left to the Royal Navy and other ships from Europe. To enable large anti-submarine helicopters to operate so far away from a shore base it would be necessary to build some sort of helicopter carrier, equipped not only with a large flat deck but also the workshops and repair facilities to keep them flying.

Out of this emerged the concept of a 'command cruiser', capable of accommodating Sea King large anti-submarine helicopters and also providing space for the elaborate command and communications equipment needed to control ships and aircraft over a wide area. Even helicopters benefit from a wide landing-area, and so the traditional island superstructure on the starboard side reappeared. However, in the prevailing climate of opinion, which held that aircraft carriers were unthinkable, the quaint euphemism 'through deck cruiser' was coined to explain away the flat deck. The first of what was to become a class of three ships, HMS *Invincible* was launched in May 1977 and joined the Fleet early in 1981.

While the design was under consideration British Aerospace was developing a naval version of the vertical takeoff Harrier, the famous 'jump-jet', to be called the Sea Harrier. The new carriers would be vastly more flexible and effective if they could embark a few strike aircraft in addition to their Sea King helicopters. Not only would the strike aircraft protect the helicopters from any attempt by hostile bombers to drive them away by firing missiles at them, but they would also be able to shoot down or drive away reconnaissance aircraft, the proverbial 'snoopers' reporting on Fleet movements. At a very early stage the requirements for a naval version of the Harrier were incorporated, even though political approval continued to be withheld, but finally the decision was made to buy 24 Sea Harriers, so that a new air group was ready for *Invincible* by the time she became operational.

TIMETABLE OF RN POLICY

PRECEDING EVENTS	64	65	66	67	68	69	70	71
	Harold Wilson PM Denis Healey Minister of Defence Labour		First Labour defence cuts	Healey proclaims 'RN will never be involved in another opposed landing'			Edward Heath PM Ends 'East of Suez' policy Conservative	

AIRCRAFT CARRIERS

ARK ROYAL
Commissioned 1955

Scheduled pay-off date

HERMES
Commissioned 1959

First refit

Laid up and converted to
Commando Carrier

CVA-01
Orders planned 1981

Project cancelled

ASW/CARRIER/CRUISER
Studies begin

HARRIER
Prototype (P 11 27)
Flies 1960

6 development
aircraft ordered

First production aircraft flies

DESTROYERS

COUNTY CLASS
First ordered 1956
Devonshire
commissioned 1962

Norfolk and **Antrim**
laid down

Norfolk and **Antrim**
commissioned
Completes class of 8 ships

TYPE 82
First of proposed group
of 4 ships ordered

Bristol
laid down Rest of group cancelled in favour of Type 42

TYPE 42
Design for a replacement
for Type 82 begins

Sheffield
laid down

FRIGATES

TYPE 12
First 9 ships
ordered 1955-56
commissioned
1960-61

ROTHESAY CLASS

All ships altered to take Wasp helicopter and Seacat

LEANDER CLASS

Last 3 Rothesay
hulls redesigned
as Leander Class

Danae
commissioned Completes class of 16 ships

BROAD BEAMED LEANDER **Andromeda**
launched

TYPE 81
Ordered 1955-56
Ashanti
commissioned
1961

TRIBAL CLASS **Zulu**
commissioned
Completes class of 7 ships

TYPE 21
Vosper Thornycroft given
design contract

Amazon
laid down

MISSILES

SEASLUG
First flew 1951
Trials 1959-61

First operational in
Devonshire 1962

Mk 2 operational in **Glamorgan**

Antrim last ship
built to take missile, completed

SEACAT
Ordered 1955
Trials 1960

First operational
in **Barrosa** 1962

SEA DART
Development begins
1963

First test fired

SEAWOLF
Project definition begins

First firing

EXOCET
Development begins

First firing

RN Orders
300 rounds

73	74	75	76	77	78	79	80	81	PROJECTED EVENTS

Margaret Thatcher PM
John Nott announces heavy Navy cuts
Invincible sale to Australia agreed

Labour

Conservative

PROJECTED EVENTS

Refit and retained   Actually paid-off   Last Navy squadrons of Phantoms, Buccaneers and Gannets disbanded

Serves as Commando and Anti-submarine Carrier   Minor refit   Fitted with ski-jump   Proposed pay-off date 1983

Invincible laid down   **Invincible** launched   **Illustrious** commissioned   New **Ark Royal** 1985

American AV-8B variant ordered for US Marine Corps and RAF 1982

Blue Fox radar developed   ▼ FRS.1 SEA HARRIER   25 aircraft ordered   10 ordered   First three squadrons formed

Norfolk receives Exocet

Bristol commissioned

Sheffield commissioned   ▽ ▽ ▽STRETCHED 42   **Manchester** laid down   **Liverpool** commissioned   Completes group of 10 ships

4 to be built to 1984

Scheduled out-of-service date 1985-86

...nder first to receive IKARA   **Phoebe** first to receive Exocet   Scheduled out-of-service date 1988-89

...adne
...nched Completes class of 10 ships   **Andromeda** first Seawolf conversion   Scheduled out-of-service date 1985-90

Amazon commissioned   **Avenger** Completes group of 8 ships   Estimated to be laid up 1988-

PE 22 ...sign begins   **Broadsword** ordered   **Broadsword** commissioned   ▼ STRETCHED 22   **Boxer** completing   Class of 8 planned

4 further ships ordered

Planned to phase out 1983

Avenger last ship to be fitted

First operational ...n **Bristol**   ▽ ▽ Mk 2 GWS.31 announced   GWS.31 cancelled ■

Sea trials in **Penelope**   Fitted to **Broadsword**

Fitted to **Norfolk**   ▽ **MM-40** first fired by French Navy

The end of a great ship. When HMS *Ark Royal* was stripped and sold for scrap the Royal Navy lost her powerful Phantom and Buccaneer strike aircraft as well as the airborne early warning radar cover given by her Gannets.

The Sea Harrier turned out to be a great improvement over the original ground-support version. The cockpit was redesigned to reduce the amount of work done by the pilot, and making navigation much easier, and most important of all, the new Blue Fox radar provided vastly improved weapon aiming. All these improvements have enabled the Sea Harrier to operate over the sea in all weathers, but its principal asset remains its superlative manoeuvrability. Although outclassed in sheer speed by many combat aircraft at high altitude, the Sea Harrier has proved remarkably manoeuvrable at low altitude, and has repeatedly shot down Mirage IIIs in the Falklands conflict.

A vital weakness

There remained, however, one crucial gap in the Fleet Air Arm's defences. When the last big carrier, the immortal *Ark Royal*, was taken out of service at the end of 1978 she took with her the last flight of Gannet Airborne Early Warning (AEW) aircraft. The ungainly Gannets carried a long-range surveillance radar, and by taking it out some distance from the Fleet and up to medium altitude they provided an all-round picture of hostile ships and aircraft.

The 'radar-horizon' from a surface ship is always limited by the curvature of the earth, whereas an AEW radar extends this horizon by a hundred miles or more. Of course enemy aircraft can try to shoot down the AEW aircraft, but they can be protected by the Fleet's aircraft. In air-defence AEW gives the Fleet early warning of the approach of hostile aircraft—direction and altitude—and permits the defending aircraft to get into position in good time.

Sadly successive governments refused to authorize any sort of AEW aircraft; several solutions are possible, even an AEW version of the Sea King, but nothing has been done about it. The main difficulty is that both the *Invincible* class and the older carrier *Hermes* have no catapults or arrester wires, and so they could not launch or recover a heavy aircraft like the Gannet. It would be quite feasible to fit a lightweight radar into a commercial aircraft, but the *Invincible* and *Hermes* both have 'ski-jump' ramps fitted; they enable Sea Harriers to take off with a greater load of fuel or munitions aboard, but they would prevent conventional aircraft from using the flight deck.

It might also be possible to modify the American successor to the Harrier, the AV-8B, but once again, the necessary studies have not been authorized.

How airborne early warning radar provides warships with more information and sooner. The 'lobes' of a warship's air warning radar are limited by the height of the array above water, and the curvature of the earth (exaggerated in the illustration). The airborne radar covers a wider arc and is also mobile.

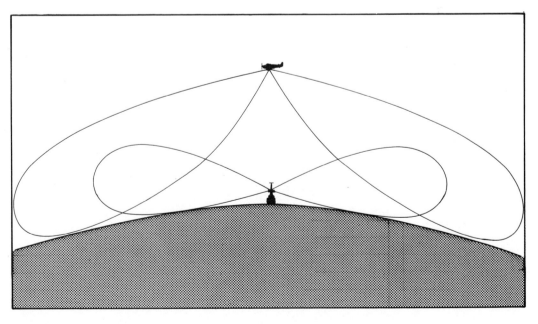

The Royal Navy has thus done its best to undo the mistakes of the mid-1960s by getting fixed-wing aircraft back to sea, but it has only been allowed to get into what might be termed the 'Second Division' of naval flying. The *Invincible* class were never intended to be attack carriers, despite claims made by politicians who saw them as a cheap solution. Moreover, the carrier *Invincible*, less than three years old, was to be sold to Australia and the newly fitted *Hermes* was 'under offer' to India. This would have left only two carriers in service by 1985, the *Illustrious* and *Ark Royal*, and the normal cycle of refits and repairs would have meant only one available for most of the time.

The amphibious capability and the Fleet's ability to replenish at sea would have been slashed as well. The assault ship *Intrepid* was to be sold (to Argentina of all countries) and two replenishment ships, the *Tidepool* and *Tidespring* had already been sold.

It is apparent to any outside observer that the Royal Navy had a more potent surface fleet in 1978 than it has in 1982, and that if the Falklands Crisis had materialised only six months later there would have been no way of sending a balanced task force to the South Atlantic.

Chapter 2
The Eve of
Battle

The fight to preserve the air element of the Royal Navy has already been described, but it was only part of the broader requirement to build surface escorts capable of defending whatever sort of aircraft carriers the Navy had, to sink submarines and to escort merchant ships.

The nomenclature of modern warships has changed over the years. In the days of sail, frigates were powerful single-decked warships capable of operating independently (cruizing) but not strong enough to fight in the line of battle. In the latter days of the 19th Century the term was replaced by cruiser, a term which embraced very large ships corresponding to 2nd Class battleships, right down to small, lightly armed scouting vessels little better than gunboats. After the First World War cruisers were broken down into heavy and light types, depending on whether they had 8-in guns or lighter, and some attempt was made to restrict their size and numbers.

The term frigate might have remained in limbo had not the Royal Navy chosen to revive it in 1943 for a new class of anti-submarine escort built for the Battle of the Atlantic. After the war all categories of escort destroyers, corvettes and sloops were lumped together as frigates, and the term was henceforward to be reserved for single-mission ships; the destroyer is so-called because she has a dual role of anti-aircraft and anti-submarine escort and her mission is to destroy all threats to the force. Thus a Type 42 destroyer may actually be smaller than a Type 22 frigate.

At the time of the Korean War production began of a new

HMS *Yarmouth*, one of nine *Rothesay* class anti-submarine frigates developed from the original *Whitby* class (Type 12) frigates in the late 1950s. *Yarmouth* was launched in March 1959 and completed in March 1960, and was refitted to carry a Wasp helicopter and Seacat close-range anti-aircraft missiles in 1966-72. She is also armed with two 4.5-in guns and triple-barrelled anti-mortars. The Type 12 hull was an outstanding success, both in the RN and in overseas navies, and was further modified to create the 26 *Leander* class ships.

series of frigates, intended to deal with the latest Russian submarines. They needed speed and weatherliness in order to be able to pursue submerged contacts, even in bad weather and the design emphasized a sustained speed of 28 knots (31.8 mph), rather than a more impressive smooth-water speed.

The series started with the *Whitby* class in the mid-1950s, and their revolutionary Type 12 hull proved so successful that it was copied for nine more *Rothesay* class which followed. Then the design was expanded to include more sophisticated equipment, mainly a long-range air-warning radar and a light helicopter, the result being the *Leander* class. In all 26 of these magnificent ships were built, and their successful sales abroad reflected other navies' appreciation of their qualities.

Criticism of design

There was, however, growing criticism of the official design team at Bath, and it was widely claimed that a private design might be able to achieve much the same result at lower cost, and with better prospects of export sales. It was even claimed by some of the private shipbuilders that a *Leander* class frigate costing £5 million (in 1964 prices) could be matched by a private design costing only £3.5 million. Clearly such a claim was worth investigating, and in 1969 the first of eight Type 21 frigates was ordered.

Unfortunately the design process proved much more complicated than the two firms had anticipated, and a bitter dispute arose between the Navy's Ship Department and the two firms concerned. The builders, Vosper Thornycroft and Yarrows, wished to use aluminium to save weight in order to achieve a reasonable payload of weapons and radars without permitting the size of the hull to rise excessively, whereas the official designers felt that aluminium was too fragile and liable to melt. The problem was not how to resist a direct hit from bombs or guided missiles, for all experience showed that no unarmoured structure could resist the impact of a ton or two of missile or a hardened nose-cone, but the need to protect against minor damage.

The risk with any modern warship is that a small explosion nearby can knock out the sensitive electronics on board and thus render a warship useless; a steel structure will offer more resistance to such blast-effects than one made of aluminium. The other great risk is the sailor's traditional nightmare, fire. As aluminium melts at about 600° C, as against about 1500° for steel, it was felt that a small fire starting accidentally might cause the

structure to collapse. If ladderways melt and decks give way the task of firefighters becomes impossible, and it is also difficult to get wounded men to safety.

Under normal circumstances the argument would not have arisen, for rigorous Ministry standards ruled out the use of aluminium structures, but in this instance the private builders had political support, and so the normal rules were set aside. But what was ultimately to prove more disastrous was a restriction on the length and beam of the hull—presumably to maintain the fiction that more could be achieved on a given tonnage than the designers of the *Leander* class had achieved.

The truth is that the *Leander* had turned out to be the better design; although designed a full 10 years earlier than the Type 21 it achieved rather more on the same tonnage and roughly the same dimensions. For example, the *Leanders* carried a long-range air-

HMS *Antelope*, one of eight *Amazon* class Type 21 frigates built in 1966–78 in an attempt to incorporate commercial standards into RN designs. It had been hoped to achieve a major improvement over the contemporary Admiralty *Leander* design and at significantly less cost. However, they cost a lot more and although comfortable and popular, proved too small to incorporate later improvements.

warning radar, whereas the Type 21 had none, despite being the same length and slightly beamier. The only advantages of the Type 21 frigate were that it was faster, thanks to gas turbine propulsion, and it had a greater degree of internal comfort, thanks to a reduced number of crew.

The reason for the success of the *Leander* design is not through any greater competence of layout, but because of the margins which have crept into official designs. Over 80 years ago the Admiralty Board introduced the so-called 'Board Margin' to permit a 10 per cent growth during the design process, and over the years official designers (in other countries as well) have developed the habit of allowing small margins in various areas of the design. This made sense because in the time taken to build a ship superior weaponry and materiél could be developed which needed to be incorporated to improve the defence of the ship.

Commercial designers, on the other hand, normally work with weapons, machinery and fittings that already exist and whose weights are already known. They therefore dispense with such margins, not least because of financial stringencies. Export customers for commercially designed ships are also unlikely to be able to afford a mid-life reconstruction, and so there is even less incentive to leave margins for future growth. The result can be, in these days of rapid developments in weaponry, a ship whose defence is out of date when it leaves the launch pad.

Only later did the drawbacks of the Type 21 become apparent. When completed all eight ships carried a quadruple Seacat missile launcher, but by the early 1970s this was recognised to be inadequate against modern aircraft. The more efficient successor was the Seawolf missile system, with the added attraction of being fast enough to cope with guided missiles; but insufficient margin had been left in the Type 21 design to allow for it. In contrast the last 10 *Leander* class frigates had been built with an extra 2 ft of beam, and they proved capable of receiving not only Seawolf but a new long-range sonar as well.

After five different schemes were examined and rejected it was reluctantly decided by 1979, only five years after the lead-ship HMS *Amazon* had entered service, that the eight ships were not worth modernizing. To make matters worse, the boast about cheaper cost was not fulfilled; instead of a cost of £3.5 million the *Amazon* was delivered at a cost of £14 million and her sisters came no cheaper. Nor did the export orders materialize, as the Australians backed out of a commitment to build five.

The new destroyer

There was also an urgent requirement for a new anti-aircraft destroyer to protect the Fleet. When the doomed carrier *CVA-01* was on the drawing board in 1966 plans were also prepared for a new class of four large guided missile-armed destroyers (DLGs). These Type 82 destroyers would have a new British medium-range (40m) guided missile and an Anglo-Australian anti-submarine missile known as Ikara. In the event the cost proved too high; only one was built, HMS *Bristol*, and the Ship Department designers were told to draw up a new smaller and cheaper design, to be known as Type 42.

It was also felt that a large fleet escort like the 6000-ton *Bristol* was no longer needed as the carriers she was supposed to escort would have disappeared by 1972. Instead the Royal Navy could make do with a ship of nearly half the tonnage. The *Bristol* design was estimated to cost £30 million (at 1966-67 prices), but as part of a cost-cutting exercise the designers were told to see how much they could achieve for a price of only £20 million.

Although any attempt to keep costs of military equipment down must be applauded, care must be taken not to achieve the ultimate waste of building a ship which cannot perform her function adequately. The political directives to the Type 42 design team came close to this, for it was decided to leave out a close-range (point-defence) missile system, even the elderly Seacat system given to the Type 21, and to make the maximum savings on internal space. A plea for slightly greater length and beam to accommodate the equipment was overruled by the Controller, in full knowledge that his refusal to permit the addition of 30 ft to the length would account for no more than 0.5 per cent increase in cost. Everything was economy-scale in the Type 42: one anchor, one galley, one workshop and even one accommodation ladder.

It was my privilege to visit the lead-ship HMS *Sheffield* just before she commissioned in March 1975 and I can well remember the compactness of her layout. Captain Heath told me that absolutely no addition to the armament could be made without sacrificing the two boats amidships—proof of how tight a margin of stability she had. A total of ten ships were built before sanity prevailed, and finally a 'Stretched 42' was authorized in 1978. All four of these ships are currently afloat and the first, HMS *Manchester* has just been completed.

Unfortunately they are still without any point-defence system, for the extra volume was only to provide more space and to improve seakeeping. However, recent events in the Falklands will result in some form of close-in defence, probably the American Phalanx 'Gatling' gun already fitted to HMS *Illustrious*.

The Navy's strengths

So far the story has been one of political interference in technical matters better left to people qualified to do the job, but the Royal Navy did manage to shake itself free. The *Invincible* class support carriers already mentioned did not suffer from restrictions on size (apart from an overall limit on the size of their air group, of course), and they have deliberately been given space for future additions.

Nor were their accompanying anti-submarine frigates, the Type 22 *Broadsword* class any different. Once again the critics of official designs voiced their criticism of the *Broadsword*, claiming that she was too big, ignoring the fact that she is intended to work

In 1974 the first order for a new type of anti-submarine frigate, the *Broadsword* class or Type 22, was placed. They are very large to provide space for a new long-range sonar, two Lynx helicopters and the Seawolf point-defence missile system. HMS *Brilliant* (below), the third of the class, was the first to fire the Seawolf in anger. The forward six-cell launcher is visible in the foreground of the photograph. HMS *Brazen*, the fourth of the class, was delivered on June 15, three months ahead of schedule.

with the *Invincible* in the North Atlantic throughout the year. Nor is she too small to carry the Seawolf anti-aircraft missile system, having two trackers and two sets of missiles, one at either end of the ship. The *Broadsword* and three sisters have joined the Fleet since 1979, and a further four, lengthened to accommodate a new, advanced towed sonar, are currently under construction.

In the past 25 years the Royal Navy has quietly been changing from the traditional method of steam propulsion to gas turbines. In 1963 the first of a class of large guided missile-armed destroyers (DLGs) went to sea with combined steam-and-gas turbines, and 11 years later HMS *Amazon* became the first operational unit with Olympus and Tyne aero-derived gas turbines. This installation has been such a success that all current frigates and destroyers use the same package, while the *Invincible* class run on four Olympus, making them the world's largest gas turbine-driven warships.

Before long the next generation of engine, the Spey will be in service, promising greater economies. Gas turbines are light, easy to run and offer rapid starting and acceleration, all considerable advantages for the warship designer.

Warfare below the surface of the sea has changed as dramatically as it has above. For many years after the Second World War anti-submarine escorts were equipped with a medium-range sensor, once known as Asdic but later called sonar to conform to American practice. The sonar transducer emitted a high-frequency 'ping' which bounced off an underwater object just like a radar-echo. Once located the submarine could then be attacked with depth-charges or homing torpedoes.

It was recognized that big helicopters from carriers or shore bases could 'dunk' a sonar or drop weapons on a submerged contact, but in the mid-1950s the British and Canadians began to experiment with helicopters operating from destroyers and frigates. The Canadians decided to stick to the Sea King, preferring to build larger destroyer escorts, but the British developed the ultra-light Wasp helicopter, capable of dropping torpedoes much further out than the frigate's depth-charge mortars could reach.

In the 1960s many frigates were fitted with hangars and flight decks to operate Wasps, and now the Anglo-French Lynx is replacing the Wasp. The helicopter has become the standard method of delivering anti-submarine weapons for the simple reason that it has more than enough speed to catch the fastest submarine, whereas in rough weather the surface warship cannot maintain full speed.

In addition to the helicopter-borne weapons the frigates and destroyers are armed with their own tubes for launching homing torpedoes. The American Mk 46 acoustic torpedo has been in service for some years but it is currently being replaced by the British Stingray. These torpedoes are smaller and lighter than the standard weapons used in submarines, and are therefore called lightweights.

Inevitably the most spectacular advance in the Royal Navy has been in the field of nuclear propulsion. Since 1963, when HMS *Dreadnought* joined the Fleet, another 11 nuclear hunter-killer submarines have been built, in addition to four Polaris-armed strategic submarines, and another six are building. Unlike the Polaris boats, whose task is to keep well away from trouble, the hunter-killers are the Royal Navy's major offensive units. They are armed with 21-in heavyweight Tigerfish wire-guided torpedoes, but will soon receive the American Sub-Harpoon anti-ship missile as well, giving them even more hitting power.

Although the nuclear submarine, with its ability to cruise continuously at high speed, is a most potent weapon, there is still a vital role for the conventional diesel-electric type. Whereas the 'nukes' make a lot of noise when running fast, and are large sonar targets, the diesel-electric boats can run very silently, and are much harder to find. In practice nuclear submarines tend to stick to traditional ambush-tactics, and only use their high speed to get clear after they have been detected.

The diesel-electric boat, on the other hand, has to come up for air frequently, and can be detected when she is 'snorkelling', either by devices which pick up infra-red emissions from her diesel exhaust or by radar detecting her snorkel mast. Modern sonar achieves phenomenal detection-ranges when used passively, for sound travels long distances through water, and the latest sonars are designed to take advantage of this.

Thus, on the eve of the battle, the Royal Navy had an uneasy mixture of strengths and weaknesses which were to be severely tested in the months to come. But in fairness its performance must be measured against the role in which it had hitherto been *expected* to function. Denis Healey said in 1966, 'the Royal Navy will never again have to make an opposed landing', a prophecy which could only remain valid if the Navy was never again called upon to act outside European waters.

Chapter 3
The Task Force Sails

The Falkland Islands were first discovered in 1592 by the English Captain John Davis, and were noted as uninhabited. The first attempt to explore them was made nearly a century later, by John Strong in 1690, and from 1706 to 1714 parties of French Breton sailors spent some time there. It is from these sporadic occupations that the island took its name *Les Malouines*—the sailors were from St Malo—and subsequently Spanish chartmakers translated the term as 'Los Islas Malvinas'.

In 1764 Bougainville attempted to found a settlement on East Falkland and claimed the islands for France, but a year later the British Commodore Byron made a rival claim to West Falkland, and a British colony was established at Port Egmont. In 1767 both claims were brushed aside by Spain, who demanded possession on the grounds that the islands were no more than an offshoot of mainland South America, and were therefore part of her colonial possessions.

The French accepted with good grace and 'sold' their settlement at Port Louis back to Spain, but it took a Spanish military operation to force the British to surrender Port Egmont in 1770. This action by the Governor of Buenos Aires was repudiated by Spain after strong British protests, and Port Egmont was returned to the British, and even when Lord North withdrew the garrison in 1774 (as part of a series of defence cuts) the claim was reiterated. In 1810 the long struggle for independence from Spain began with the declaration of an Argentine republic in Buenos Aires, and Spain withdrew its garrison from the Malvinas.

Sea Harriers and Sea Kings crowded aboard the *Hermes* flight deck as she leaves on April 5. Note the combat fuel tanks on the inner pylons of the Harriers and the tie-downs securing the aircraft to the deck.

In 1820 the Argentine ship *Heroina* sailed to Port Louis to claim the islands for Argentina, a claim which was disputed diplomatically by the British, but with no military counteraction to enforce it. Ironically the first military action to be taken against the Argentine colonists was by the United States in 1831 when Commodore Duncan in the corvette *Lexington* sacked the settlement, and a year later the British Government took the first steps to reassert their rights.

On February 2, 1831 HMS *Clio* and HMS *Tyne* forced the small Argentine garrison to surrender and hoisted the Union flag once more. From then until 1914 the islands were left undisturbed; a population of English settlers grew to about 2000, subsisting on sheep farming, with little or no contact with the outside world.

The Battle of the Falklands in November 1914 showed that the islands had strategic value as a naval coaling station and telegraph link, a point which was proved again in December 1939, when the heavy cruiser HMS *Cumberland* carried out essential repairs at Port Stanley during the Battle of the River Plate.

Not until 1945 did Argentina re-open the question of sovereignty, and since then it has become a matter of growing acrimony. During the reign of General Peron the repossession of Las Malvinas was turned into a national aspiration, with school children reciting the story every day, whereas in Britain only a handful of people showed any interest in the Falklands. As pressure from Argentina grew more strident a few warning voices were heard, reminding the British Government that the Falklands would have to be defended if it was felt vital to keep them.

The alternative was to find a way to cede the islands back to Argentina, but this was hampered by a continuing instability in Argentine politics, culminating in the notorious takeover by the military, in which thousands of civilians disappeared, apparently murdered by army and police 'death squads'.

As recently as 1977 there was a direct threat by the military in Buenos Aires to solve the 'Malvinas Question' by force. This was countered by a mixture of bluff and discreet use of the Royal Navy by the then Labour Government, which was ordered to mount an 'exercise' in the South Atlantic. Even more successful was the stationing of nuclear submarines off the principal naval bases, and the crisis was kept under control, virtually unnoticed by the civilian population, either in Argentina or Britain. Unfortunately it led to complacency, with the result that the British

Portsmouth

EQUATOR

ASCENSION
ISLAND

ARGENTINA

Buenos Montevedeo
Aires

FALKLAND
ISLANDS

SOUTH
GEORGIA

0   600   1200
MILES

diplomats were under the illusion that peaceful negotiations could continue, and that military threats could be ignored.

The Argentines, recognizing that the British wished to get rid of the Falklands, pursued a 'hearts and minds' campaign, helping with secondary education, hospital treatment, and even running a civilian airline to Port Stanley, but it failed to make any headway against a deep-rooted suspicion among the Falklanders, who wished to pursue their remote but simple and uncomplicated lives without change.

Although it now looks obvious, the Argentine seizure of the islands came as a thunderclap. On Friday April 2 the British press carried reports from Argentina, claiming that an invasion of the islands and the South Georgia Dependency was under way. A dazed Government and Foreign Office frantically tried to obtain confirmation of these reports, and by the following day TV film was available showing Argentine armoured vehicles in the streets of Port Stanley.

Whatever the legal position Great Britain was clearly responsible as the legal protector of the 1800 islanders, and the United Nations recognized this by drafting Resolution No 502, calling on Argentina to withdraw her troops immediately.

Like so many UN resolutions No 502 was ignored, and so Great Britain announced her intention of dispatching a large naval task force to secure the withdrawal of Argentine forces. As part of this reassertion of her rights Britain declared a 200-mile Exclusion Zone around the Falklands and South Georgia, in which Argentine ships would be treated as hostile. In the short term this blockade could only be enforced by whatever submarines could be sent to the area.

In the meantime all that could be done was to get together as many ships, aircraft and troops as could be found, and organize the logistical nightmare of sending them 8000 miles down into the South Atlantic. Bear in mind also that it was Easter, and thanks to an apparent oversight by someone in Whitehall (possibly on the advice of that same Foreign Office which had failed to read anything into intelligence reports of the invasion) roughly half of the sailors of the Fleet had been given Easter leave.

The Argentine forces

At the time of the invasion, the total force of aircraft and helicopters in Argentine service (in addition to the Air Force, both the Navy and Army maintained air arms) amounted to nearly 700.

Many of these were approaching obsolescence, but that must not be taken to assume impotence. On paper, and in the event, Argentine air power was a formidable threat.

Not unnaturally, the *Fuerza Aerea Argentina* (the Argentine Air Force) was the major air arm of the forces. Her inventory boasted nearly 540 aircraft, of which some 190 were front-line operational combat types. The most numerous was the McDonnell Douglas A-4P Skyhawk, of which 64 out of the 75 originally delivered in 1966-67 remained in use. The Skyhawk was originally designed as a lightweight bomber for the US Navy and the A-4P variants in Argentine service were refurbished and updated ex-US Navy A-4Bs and A-4Cs.

The most modern fighter in the Air Force line-up was the Mirage III, of which two versions were in service; the Dassault Mirage IIIEA and the Israel Aircraft Industries (IAI) Nesher (or Dagger). Between 1972 and 1980 Argentina received 21 Mirage IIIs and when the Falklands was invaded some 19 IIIEs were thought to be in use.

Although bought for interceptor duties, the Mirage IIIEs were designed for, and in the event used as long-range fighter-

An Argentine Navy A-4Q Skyhawk with underwing fuel tanks, prepares to load 3 2000-lb bombs. The Skyhawks had the facility for inflight refuelling through the probe along the nose.

bombers. The IIIEA is capable of speeds in excess of Mach 2 (twice the speed of sound) at 39 000 ft, but this speed was reduced when the aircraft was forced to operate in a fighter-bomber role at low level and at the limit of its combat range (which happened during the conflict). In these circumstances all an opponent had to do was to make the pilot engage his afterburner, doubling the use of fuel and ensuring that the aircraft could not return to base.

The other 'Mirage' in Argentine service, the IAI Nesher (known as the Dagger by the Argentines) was the Israeli copy of the Mirage IIICJ. It was fitted with Israeli electronic, avionic and other equipment. This version is thought to have flown for the first time in September 1969, and Argentina took delivery of 26 Daggers between 1978 and 1979.

The Argentine bomber force (in the traditional sense, as opposed to fighter-bombers or attack aircraft) was composed of eight British Aerospace Canberra B.62s delivered in 1970-1971.

The fifth major combat aircraft in the Argentine Air Force was the indigenously designed and built IA.58 Pucará. This two-seat, straight-wing ground-attack aircraft was unconventional for its role, being powered by a pair of turboprops, giving it a maximum speed of 320 mph. However, it was capable of packing a very heavy punch, as British forces found out during the conflict.

Designed to take part in counter-insurgency operations, its slow speed enabled it to deliver its weapon load accurately and to use its guns for a strafing role. When the conflict started it was thought that 75 out of over 80 Pucarás delivered were in use.

Argentina was also one of two countries in South America (the other is Brazil) which had an aircraft carrier—the *Vienticinco de Mayo* (formerly HMS *Venerable*) and naval air operations were controlled by the *Comando de Aviacion Naval Argentina*. Although the naval air arm comprised nearly 130 aircraft, only 18 combat aircraft were available at the outset of hostilities; despite the fact that some (if not all) of the Aermacchi MB.339A trainers in service were used as light strike aircraft from Port Stanley.

The combat element of the *Vienticinco de Mayo*'s air group consisted of 12 Douglas A-4Q Skyhawks—basically the same as the A-4P described earlier. The anti-submarine warfare (ASW) element of the air group comprised four Grumman S-2E Trackers and four Sikorsky SH-3D Sea King helicopters. However, the carrier, mysteriously, never went to sea after the invasion and thus never really fought her potentially powerful air group.

The most important Argentine naval aircraft, the one which

HMS *Invincible* (*overleaf*), the first of a new class of aircraft carriers, was a vital element of the Task Force. HMS *Hermes*, although an older carrier, was made flagship, and these two photographs show her men hard at work and relaxing. In the foreground of the hangar (*above*) marines check their kit, while maintainers work on aircraft and a helicopter in the background. On Easter Sunday, April 11, they enjoy the sun (*right*) before heading into the South Atlantic autumn. *Hermes* carried a crew of nearly 1000 with an additional 1000 Royal Marine Commandos. Keeping fit and getting battle-ready in the cramped space between decks as the weather got increasingly bad on deck became a worrying problem for the land commanders.

On board the *Invincible* and *Hermes*, the aircraft provided air cover and the helicopters protection against submarine attack. *Above*, four FRS.1 Sea Harriers are 'spotted' on the flight deck ready for takeoff, and *(far left)* one takes off from the 'ski-jump' on *Hermes*. Views of *Invincible* in the South Atlantic *(left)* are rare. Here she is running astern of *Hermes*.

The Sea King helicopters were used extensively when the deployment of the amphibious forces started, to ferry troops. *Right*, a Sea Harrier maintains a Combat Air Patrol (CAP) in the background, while two Sea King HAS.1s hover, and one of the aircrew runs to a third, just prior to takeoff. *Above*, a Sea King on the forward flight deck of the liner *Canberra* gets ready to 'cross-deck' troops to an assault ship (*Fearless* or *Intrepid*) signalling by lamp in the background.

The results of an Exocet attack (*above*). The burnt-out hulk of the destroyer *Sheffield* abandoned after her crew had fought for hours to save her. Note the Type 966 'bedstead' radar antenna turned to starboard, the twin Sea Dart missile launcher in the loading position (but not loaded), and the areas of bare plating burned by the fires which raged out of control. Photographs of this deadly Exocet AM-39 air-launched missile are rare (*right*). It is designed for launching from the French-made Super Etendard, but is compatible with a wide range of aircraft and helicopters like this Mk 75 Sea King.

cost the Royal Navy most dearly, was the Dassault-Breguet Super Etendard, the launch aircraft for the deadly AM-39 air-launched version of the Exocet anti-ship missile. Some 14 of these aircraft were ordered from France in 1979, and when hostilities broke out six had been delivered, together with (it is thought) six AM-39 Exocets.

The Super Etendard was the most modern combat aircraft in the entire Argentine front-line, having been designed for the French *Aéronavale*. It first flew in 1974 and has a maximum level speed at low altitude of 748 mph. When fitted with the Exocet it has a radius of 450 miles. All Super Etendard operations during the conflict were conducted from land bases.

Like most navies today, the Argentine Navy also operated helicopters from other vessels, mainly destroyers and frigates. The main type in service was the Alouette III, of which nine were thought to be operational. The two British-built Type 42 destroyers each had a single Lynx HAS.23 helicopter.

Land-based maritime patrol was the responsibility of the Argentine Navy, and to undertake this task there were nine Lockheed SP-2H and SP-2E Neptunes. That being said, it is interesting to note that Air Force Boeing 707-387B airliners undertook the long-range reconnaissance missions which were met by Sea Harriers and escorted away from the British Fleet.

The Argentine Army also possessed an aviation element

The Argentine-built Pucará counter-insurgency aircraft proved its worth in numerous attacks on British land forces, and it was even used to attack shipping. It was armed with 2 20-mm cannon and 4 7.62-mm machine guns. This photograph shows three 500-lb bombs on the centreline pylon with two rocket pads on each of the wing pylons. About 75 Pucarás were in service at the start of the conflict.

comprising helicopters and communications aircraft for army support duties. The main types in service were the Aérospatiale SA.315 Lama, SA.330L Puma, the Agusta A.109A, the Bell UH-lH Iroquois (or Huey) and the Boeing-Vertol CH-47C Chinook. There were also three Aeritalia G222 transports which could well have been involved in resupply missions to the Falklands after their occupation—carrying 44 troops or 20 945 lb of cargo.

The Argentine Navy (*Armada Republica Argentina*) was in the throes of modernization. In addition to refurbishing the carrier *Vienticinco de Mayo*, four new frigates, six corvettes and four submarines were under construction.

These were to replace the 44-year-old cruiser *General Belgrano* (15 6-in guns, 11 000 tons), nine old American destroyers and two old American submarines. Apart from these veterans of the Second World War there were also two Type 42 destroyers (one built in Britain and one built locally), the *Hercules* and *Santisima Trinidad*, and two German-built submarines, the *Salta* and *San Luis*. The unprepared state of her Navy possibly gives a good indication that the Argentines did not expect Britain to fight.

Argentina invades
The initial air support for the Argentine invasion of the Falklands came from the carrier *Vienticinco de Mayo*, and Army helicopters deployed with their Fleet. Early on April 2, 150 Argentine marine special forces were landed by helicopters (thought to be SH-3D Sea Kings and possibly Pumas) near the Royal Marine barracks at Moody Brook, outside Port Stanley.

After the port had been secured, C-130 Hercules transports of the Argentine Air Force began landing at Port Stanley airport, and the build-up of forces on the islands had begun.

During the capture of South Georgia, Alouette IIIs of the Argentine Navy and at least one Army Puma were used, being based on the ice-patrol vessel *Bahia Pariso* and the corvette *Granville*. During the landing, the 22-strong Royal Marine detachment landed on South Georgia by the *Endurance* on March 31 severely damaged one Puma, causing it to crash, and shot down one Alouette III. The Puma was hit by a Carl Gustav anti-tank rocket (which also holed the *Granville* below the waterline) and the Alouette III was brought down by small arms fire. The Argentine landing there did not go unopposed, although the 22-man detachment shortly afterwards surrendered.

With the nominal British presence in the Falklands and South Georgia neutralized, Argentina began the build-up of forces and material on the islands. Although details of the exact operations are unavailable, it may reasonably be assumed that the Air Force fleet of C-130E and C-130H Hercules and the Fokker F.27 Friendships bore the brunt of the aerial re-supply, possibly assisted by the Army's G222 transports.

Britain prepares to act

There were many who doubted that the hardened arteries of the Ministry of Defence could pump blood fast enough to react to such a crisis, but slowly it began to dawn on everyone that the British meant what they had said. While the unwelcome news of the surrender of the tiny garrisons of Royal Marines at Port Stanley and South Georgia was being digested the carriers *Invincible* and *Hermes* were preparing to set sail, their decks packed with vehicles, Sea King helicopters and Sea Harriers.

Amid emotional scenes the *Invincible* and *Hermes* left Portsmouth on Monday April 5. Their commander was 49-year-old Rear Admiral John ('Sandy') Woodward, a former submariner whose current post was Flag Officer, First Flotilla—known in Navy slang as 'FOF 1'.

It is a bizarre coincidence that in November 1914 another *Invincible* had set sail for the Falklands, to avenge a British defeat at the hands of a German cruiser-squadron under Vice Admiral Graf Spee. She and her sister *Inflexible* had arrived just in time to save Port Stanley from occupation and had immediately won a resounding victory over the armoured cruisers *Scharnhorst* and *Gneisenau*. Few could fail to be moved by the fact that HMS *Invincible*'s battle honours include the proud 'Falklands 1914'.

The main element of British air power used during the Falklands conflict came from the Fleet Air Arm, based on the two aircraft carriers deployed with the Task Force, of which HMS *Hermes* was named flagship, as well as the many helicopters on the other ships of the Fleet.

The Royal Air Force's role in the conflict was mainly one of providing support, although a number of their ground-attack Harrier GR.3s supplemented the Navy's Sea Harriers; and the Vulcan B.2 bomber which, in the twilight of its RAF service, went into action for the first time on May 1, 1982, attacking the Port Stanley airfield, and opening the way for military action to retake the Falklands.

The two aircraft carriers *Hermes* and *Invincible* leaving Portsmouth on May 5. HMS *Hermes* (*top*) was made flagship. She served as a fixed-wing carrier from 1959 to 1970, and so was the last link with the Old Navy. In 1973 she returned to active service as a commando carrier, operating only helicopters. In 1977 she was switched to the anti-submarine role. In 1981 she emerged from a major refit with a 12° 'ski-jump' to operate the first Sea Harrier squadron. Orders to sail had been given to both carriers only three days before they sailed.

The prime aircraft on the British side was the British Aerospace Sea Harrier FRS.1 of the Fleet Air Arm. The Royal Navy ordered the Sea Harrier in 1975, and by the end of April 1982, all 34 aircraft on order had been delivered. Some 30 Sea Harriers were eventually thought to have been deployed in the South Atlantic, though 19 sailed with the two carriers initially. Three squadrons were equipped with the type; 800 Sqn in *Hermes* and 801 Sqn in *Invincible*, while 899 Sqn's aircraft were split between the two carriers. A fourth unit, 809 Sqn, was commissioned during the conflict and flew out to join the fleet at the beginning of May.

The Sea Harrier was the naval version of the world's first operational short takeoff and vertical landing (STOVL) fighter, and was thought to be outclassed by the Mirages and Daggers in Argentine service. Events proved the critics wrong and the Sea Harriers were found to be worth their weight in gold.

The Sea Harrier has a maximum speed in excess of 730 mph, and as an interceptor has a combat range of 460 miles. Its unique advantage over conventional aircraft in combat is that its vectored thrust engine can be used in flight to change the aircraft's direction radically, thus enabling it to out-manoeuvre an opponent. This is known as 'Vectored Thrust in Forward Flight' or 'Viffing'. In the event, however, it would appear (at the time of writing) that this manoeuvre was *not* used in combat, as the Sea Harrier's opponents were armed only for strike duties, and they were operating at the extreme end of their range and therefore did not have the fuel to 'mix-it' in combat with the Sea Harriers.

The principal helicopter serving with the Fleet Air Arm was

the Westland Sea King, used in two versions for the anti-submarine role (the HAS.2 and HAS.5) and troop-or-cargo-carrying (the HC.4). Three anti-submarine Sea King units were initially deployed with the Task Force; 820 Sqn, 826 Sqn and 706 Sqn (the latter was a second-line unit brought into action for the conflict).

The Sea King HC.4s of 846 Sqn were based in *Hermes*. Later in the conflict, a new Sea King unit, 825 Sqn was commissioned to sail with the *Atlantic Causeway*, after conversion to a 'mini-carrier'. Other ships in the Task Force, notably the Royal Fleet Auxiliaries (RFAs) *Fort Austin*, *Fort Grange* and *Engadine*, and possibly some others, also embarked Sea Kings singly or in pairs.

The two assault ships, HMS *Fearless* and HMS *Intrepid* embarked Westland Wessex HU.5 commando-carrying helicopters of 845 Sqn, while the *Atlantic Conveyor* took further Wessexes down to the South Atlantic.

The final elements of the Fleet Air Arm sent to the South Atlantic were the small helicopters operating from destroyers and frigates assigned to the force. Most were Westland Lynx HAS.2 helicopters, which can operate either as a platform for ASW torpedoes or in the anti-ship vessel role with AS-12 or Sea Skua anti-ship missiles. These aircraft are deployed singly or in pairs (in the Type 22 class of frigates), and all belong to 815 Sqn. The other small helicopter already mentioned is the Westland Wasp HAS.1, which equips the *Rothesay* class frigates and HMS *Endurance*, and they belong to 829 Sqn.

The RAF's contribution to the Task Force air armada was smaller but nonetheless vital. Some 14 Harrier GR.3s, drawn from

1 Sqn and 233 Operational Conversion Unit, both based at RAF Wittering, were hastily converted to carry the American AIM-9L Sidewinder air-to-air missile (AAM), the main air defence weapon of the Sea Harrier.

Like the Sea Harrier, they retained the twin 30-mm Aden cannon, and when the time came, undertook the close air support of the troops on the ground, leaving the Sea Harrier free for air-defence duties.

The Harriers arrived with the Fleet on May 8 together with 809 Sqn's Sea Harriers, after being ferried to Ascension Island, supported by Handley Page Victor K.2 tankers. Their performance and powerplant is virtually identical to the Sea Harrier, but they do not carry radar; instead the nose contains a laser Ranger and Marked Target Seeker for use in air-to-ground attack. Before leaving the UK the RAF pilots practised 'ski-jump' takeoffs from the static ramps at RAF Yeovilton, the Navy's Sea Harrier base.

Although the RAF provided considerable air support to the Task Force from Ascension Island, including the Vulcan B.2 bombers which raided Port Stanley, the only other contribution to the Task Force was the Chinook HC.1 medium-lift helicopter. Five such are known to have been sent south on board the *Atlantic Conveyor*. Flown by crews of 18 Sqn, one aircraft was left at Ascension to help the distribution of stores amongst ships calling there on their way south.

One Chinook was airborne when the *Atlantic Conveyor* was later sunk . . . 'Bravo November' and so three Chinooks are assumed to have been lost. It is reported that the single Chinook performed magnificently in the Falklands, at one stage ferrying 81 troops instead of 44, and it is interesting to note that an Argentine Chinook captured intact in the Falklands was immediately pressed into service by the RAF.

The final component of the British air forces in the Falklands conflict came from the Army Air Corps (who celebrate their Silver Jubilee in 1982). They operated a number of Westland/ Aérospatiale SA.341 Gazelle AH.1 light observation helicopters, and Westland Scout AH.1 utility helicopters.

The Task Force gathers strength

By a stroke of luck a number of warships had been on a NATO weapon training exercise off Gibraltar and so these ships were free to join the Task Force after refuelling and re-ammunitioning. There was, and still is, a great deal of secrecy surrounding the

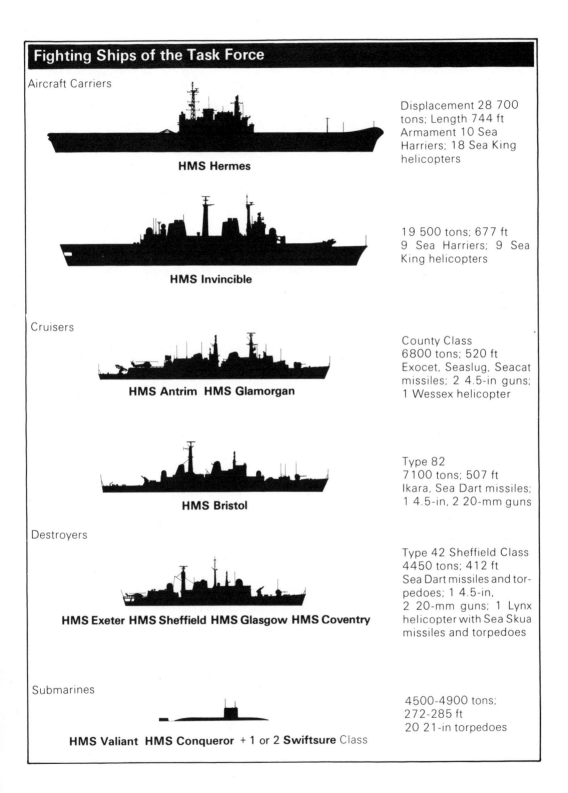

Fighting Ships of the Task Force

Aircraft Carriers

HMS Hermes

Displacement 28 700 tons; Length 744 ft Armament 10 Sea Harriers; 18 Sea King helicopters

HMS Invincible

19 500 tons; 677 ft 9 Sea Harriers; 9 Sea King helicopters

Cruisers

HMS Antrim HMS Glamorgan

County Class 6800 tons; 520 ft Exocet, Seaslug, Seacat missiles; 2 4.5-in guns; 1 Wessex helicopter

HMS Bristol

Type 82 7100 tons; 507 ft Ikara, Sea Dart missiles; 1 4.5-in, 2 20-mm guns

Destroyers

HMS Exeter HMS Sheffield HMS Glasgow HMS Coventry

Type 42 Sheffield Class 4450 tons; 412 ft Sea Dart missiles and torpedoes; 1 4.5-in, 2 20-mm guns; 1 Lynx helicopter with Sea Skua missiles and torpedoes

Submarines

HMS Valiant HMS Conqueror + 1 or 2 **Swiftsure** Class

4500-4900 tons; 272-285 ft 20 21-in torpedoes

The educational cruise-ship *Uganda* was converted to a hospital ship at Gibraltar with a helicopter deck and satellite communications terminal added; she sailed early on April 19. During the Battle of the Falklands she was moored in Falkland Sound and received casualties directly from the battlefield. At the battle's peak, after the *Sir Galahad*, *Sir Tristram* and *Plymouth* bombings and casualties, NOSH (Naval Ocean-going Surgical Hospital) as she was nicknamed by her crew, took 159 injured on board in four hours. During conversion, the cocktail bar became a path lab, the cabin passengers' smoking room an intensive care unit, and the hair-dressing salon an X-ray room.

despatch of certain warships to the Falklands. Some ships off Gibraltar (such as the Ikara-armed *Leander* class frigates *Aurora* and *Galatea*) were thought to have gone, but were then sent back to Devonport. Others, such as *Brilliant*, *Broadsword*, *Antrim*, *Alacrity*, *Sheffield*, *Glamorgan* and *Invincible* did go directly after the exercises (with *Invincible* returning to Portsmouth first). But the problem of supplying a force in the South Atlantic was if anything greater than the problem of what to do when the Task Force arrived. Feeding the 2000-odd Royal Marines and the sailors embarked in the Task Force and keeping a chain of supply from the United Kingdom 8000 miles into the South Atlantic would require more ships than the Royal Fleet Auxiliary could muster.

On the day that the Task Force sailed the luxury cruiser liner *Canberra* was requisitioned from her owners, the P & O Shipping Co. By the time she had returned from the Mediterranean to Southampton two helicopter platforms had been built on shore and were ready to be installed. The 45 000-ton ship was converted and loaded at Southampton under conditions of wartime security, and she sailed from No 8 Dock on the evening of April 9, carrying another 2000 troops.

A feature of the rapid mobilization was the number of

Fighting Ships of the Task Force

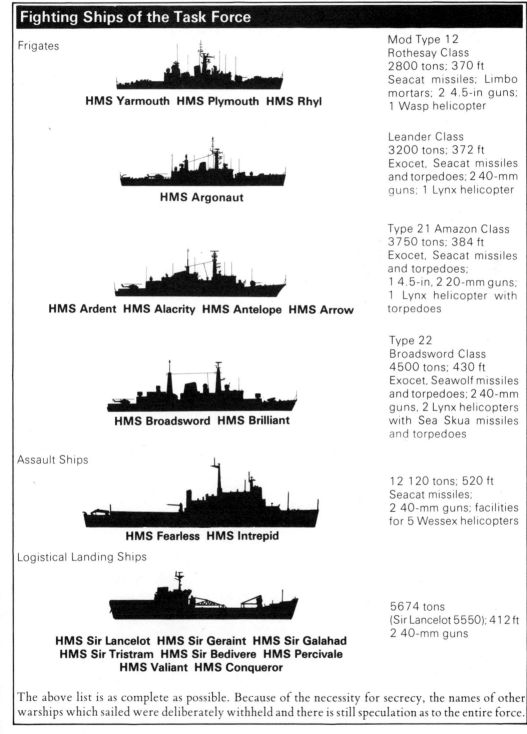

Frigates

HMS Yarmouth HMS Plymouth HMS Rhyl

Mod Type 12
Rothesay Class
2800 tons; 370 ft
Seacat missiles; Limbo
mortars; 2 4.5-in guns;
1 Wasp helicopter

HMS Argonaut

Leander Class
3200 tons; 372 ft
Exocet, Seacat missiles
and torpedoes; 2 40-mm
guns; 1 Lynx helicopter

HMS Ardent HMS Alacrity HMS Antelope HMS Arrow

Type 21 Amazon Class
3750 tons; 384 ft
Exocet, Seacat missiles
and torpedoes;
1 4.5-in, 2 20-mm guns;
1 Lynx helicopter with
torpedoes

HMS Broadsword HMS Brilliant

Type 22
Broadsword Class
4500 tons; 430 ft
Exocet, Seawolf missiles
and torpedoes; 2 40-mm
guns, 2 Lynx helicopters
with Sea Skua missiles
and torpedoes

Assault Ships

HMS Fearless HMS Intrepid

12 120 tons; 520 ft
Seacat missiles;
2 40-mm guns; facilities
for 5 Wessex helicopters

Logistical Landing Ships

**HMS Sir Lancelot HMS Sir Geraint HMS Sir Galahad
HMS Sir Tristram HMS Sir Bedivere HMS Percivale
HMS Valiant HMS Conqueror**

5674 tons
(Sir Lancelot 5550); 412 ft
2 40-mm guns

The above list is as complete as possible. Because of the necessity for secrecy, the names of other warships which sailed were deliberately withheld and there is still speculation as to the entire force.

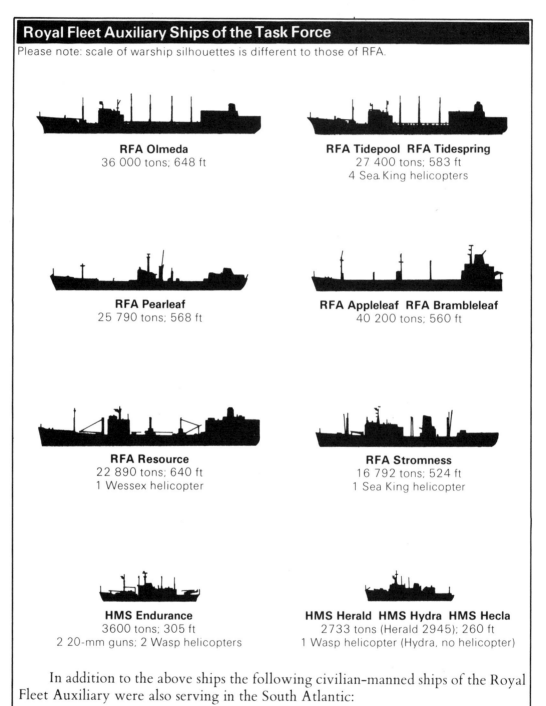

Royal Fleet Auxiliary Ships of the Task Force

Please note: scale of warship silhouettes is different to those of RFA.

RFA Olmeda
36 000 tons; 648 ft

RFA Tidepool RFA Tidespring
27 400 tons; 583 ft
4 Sea King helicopters

RFA Pearleaf
25 790 tons; 568 ft

RFA Appleleaf RFA Brambleleaf
40 200 tons; 560 ft

RFA Resource
22 890 tons; 640 ft
1 Wessex helicopter

RFA Stromness
16 792 tons; 524 ft
1 Sea King helicopter

HMS Endurance
3600 tons; 305 ft
2 20-mm guns; 2 Wasp helicopters

HMS Herald HMS Hydra HMS Hecla
2733 tons (Herald 2945); 260 ft
1 Wasp helicopter (Hydra, no helicopter)

In addition to the above ships the following civilian-manned ships of the Royal Fleet Auxiliary were also serving in the South Atlantic:

Engadine Helicopter support ship **Fort Austin Fort Grange Resource** Fleet replenishment ships **Plumleaf** Fleet oiler **Blue Rover Grey Rover** Small replenishment tankers merchant ships hastily requisitioned or chartered. Fortunately the charter market was depressed, and many ships were readily available. Roll-on/roll-off transporters, tankers and even a North Sea ferry were pressed into service. The small liner *Uganda*, which for many years had been used for educational cruises, was converted to a hospital ship at Gibraltar. (For a full list of commandeered merchant ships see Appendix C on p 136.)

The only staging post available to the British was Ascension Island, a barren volcanic outcrop 3500 miles away in the South Atlantic; although a British possession, it had for many years been leased to the United States.

The first direct military aid authorized by President Reagan was permission to use the facilities of Ascension, both as a staging post for shipborne supplies and as an airfield from which military aircraft could operate. Without that vital stepping stone the British could not even have contemplated any significant scale of military action in the South Atlantic, for they had allowed their rights to the Simon's Town base in South Africa to lapse.

Clearly there was little point in trying to enforce the blockade of the Falklands until some forces were in position and the first nuclear submarines were not on station until April 12. On that date, at 5 am (London time) the 200-mile Maritime Exclusion Zone came into effect. It was claimed by the Ministry of Defence that all the major warships of the *Armada Republica Argentina* had been withdrawn to its home ports, leaving only one destroyer and a frigate still at sea.

The threat posed by the British 'nukes' was more psychological than real, for these 4000-ton craft are too big to be risked in shallow waters, and their torpedoes are not suited to attacking small craft such as patrol boats. On the other hand, they can make their presence known, discouraging the free passage of larger ships such as transports and major warships. This had in fact been done in 1977, in a previous period of tension. A skilful combination of 'naval exercises' in the South Atlantic and the stationing of nuclear submarines off Argentina's main naval bases had been sufficient to head off an attack on the Falklands.

Life on board the Task Force

Meanwhile the Task Force was heading south. When the main body arrived at Ascension it waited to allow slower ships to catch up. The time was used to let the troops get ashore for some exercise and training.

At sea the two carriers exercised their air groups constantly. Flare targets were trailed a mile off the beam, allowing the Sea Harriers to fire Sidewinder heat-seeking missiles, or splash targets for their bombs. There was full awareness that the ships were entering a war zone, for shortly after leaving Ascension the ships detected an Argentine Boeing 707 airliner, outwardly a civilian airliner but many hundreds of miles away from any known air-route. The intruder was recognized as a 'snooper' (her search radar transmissions could be detected and identified by the ships) and two Sea Harriers chased her away, but the position of the Task Force was now known to the Argentines. These unarmed reconnaissance flights were not fired on by the British as the Total Exclusion Zone had not yet been extended to include airspace.

Aboard all ships full precautions were observed. Anti-flash hoods, gas masks and life-preservers were to be worn at all times. 'Darken Ship' routine was observed, and damage control drills were carried out to sharpen the reactions of all the various components of each ship's organization. It was reported that some of the men, such as Aircraft Electrical Mechanics (AEMs) handling Sidewinder missiles in the magazines, saw no daylight for hours. One of the minor austerities of war-conditions is the removal of napkin rings from the wardroom—if the ship were to be hit such metal objects would turn into dangerous projectiles. Mirrors and other breakable fittings have to be removed and stored, for the same reason.

As always, mail from home was the most welcome thing for the crew and troops, and this was taken care of by Nimrods and later Hercules, from Ascension, dropping waterproof canisters into the sea. A Sea King helicopter then sent a crewman, clad in a wet suit, into the water to recover the canister.

For a while the weather was very good, but as the ships ploughed steadily southwards the temperature dropped. The Falklands are on approximately the same latitude as London, lying between 51°-53° South, but without the warmth of the Gulf Stream the real British equivalent is the Outer Hebrides or the Shetlands. However the Falklands are spared the worst of the winds of the 'Roaring Forties', and the winds are often fiercer in summer than in winter. What made the Falklands climate so hard to bear was the total lack of predictability, and days of thick fog and rain could be followed by bright sunshine.

Reports from the Task Force reflected the worsening weather. Warnings about sharks began to be replaced by advice on how to survive in Antarctic conditions. All personnel on duty on the bridge or the weatherdeck were told to use chapsticks and lip-salve to protect against cold sores and cracked skin. Much worse was the risk of windchill, frostbite or hypothermia. Dire warnings were issued to dissuade people from trusting to the joys of alcohol, for after the initial glow of warmth and well-being the effects on the human body in extreme cold are disastrous. It increases the surface temperature of the skin, opening the blood vessels and causing the body temperature to fall very rapidly.

Logistical back-up

The military strength of the Task Force gave little clue to the massive logistical effort needed to support it. By April 21 it was known that at least 35 merchant ships had been chartered or requisitioned. These included in addition to the liner *Canberra* and the liner *Queen Elizabeth II*, no fewer than 20 tankers, a 20 000-ton water tanker, roll-on/roll-off (Ro-Ro) ferries, freighters and tugs. The majority of ships were used to carry fuel and dry stores to Ascension, where it was then transhipped to Navy replenishment ships, but others had a specific role to play with the Task Force.

The tugs were intended to tow damaged vessels clear of the battle zone, while the Ro-Ro ferries were intended to carry the Army vehicles, guns and heavy equipment. The *Atlantic Conveyor*, a 14 946 GRT Ro-Ro ship, was fitted with a flight deck in order to

The liner *Canberra* was converted to a troopship at Southampton and took 2000 Royal Marines down to the Falklands. This photograph, received in London on May 5, shows her refuelling from a Royal Fleet Auxiliary. The Refuelling at Sea (RAS) rig to allow *Canberra* to do this was made specially by the Royal Engineers.

provide RAF Harriers and Chinook heavy-lift helicopters with a spare deck. Five 1200-ton stern trawlers were converted to minesweepers, in case it proved necessary to sweep ground mines off Port Stanley. It was and using the latest sweep-gear they were able to sweep deep anchorages more efficiently than the normal coastal minesweepers, and were in addition better able to cope with the South Atlantic weather.

The seamen aboard the chartered and requisitioned merchant ships were paid the so-called 'war risks' bonus of 150 per cent. This bonus applied in the 'War Zone', which extended from Ascension Island south to the Falklands and South Georgia. Surprisingly this incentive scheme did not apply to the men of the Royal Fleet Auxiliary, who only received the bonus when operating within 200 miles of the coast of Argentina, the Falklands or South Georgia. Subsequently, however, the zone was extended to the estuary of the River Plate, which forms the northern sea boundary of Argentina.

The rapidity with which the crisis materialized meant that some men had no chance to exercise their right to 'sign off'. The replenishment ship *Fort Austin*, for example, was lying at Gibraltar on March 28, having just returned from six months in the Persian Gulf. Next day, just after noon the ship weighed anchor and was

Excess small arms ammunition and stores from the frigate *Brilliant* are brought aboard *Hermes* by a Lynx helicopter at Ascension. A stop-over at Ascension allowed essential transshipment of goods as well as giving time for vital last-minute training for the troops. It also permitted the slower ships to catch up with the Task Force Fleet. The Fleet sailed at an average of 28 knots, while *Canberra* sailed at 22 knots, the landing ships at 17 knots and the assault ships at 21 knots.

passing through the Straits when the Captain, Commodore Sam Dunlop, announced over the loudspeaker that fresh sailing orders had been received, and that the ship would proceed direct to the Falklands.

Some of the ships of the regular Navy also found unusual employment. Three survey ships, the *Hecla*, *Hydra* and *Herald* were converted at short notice to 'ambulance ferries', or small hospital ships to carry wounded from outlying ships to the main hospital ship, the converted liner *Uganda*. The new offshore patrol vessels *Leeds Castle* and *Dumbarton Castle* were used as despatch vessels, carrying mail between the Task Force and Ascension.

The inclusion of the giant liner *Queen Elizabeth II* came as a surprise when it was reported on April 24. Like the *Canberra* the 67 000-ton liner was rapidly fitted with helicopter flight decks, three in all, and she embarked 5 Brigade at Southampton by May 11, before sailing for the Falklands a day later. The scenes as the giant ship moved away from the quayside brought back memories of the Second World War which outdid even the emotion generated by the departure of the Task Force a month earlier. The 3000 men aboard her were an absolutely necessary ingredient of the Task Force as Argentina had made no secret of her determination to build up the garrison of the Falklands, and was reputed to have 9000 men already in position.

The main body of ships had already done a complicated 'cross-decking' operation at Ascension, sorting weapons and ammunition out among the various formations. Helicopters were used to shuttle stores from ship to ship, while the troops were sent ashore to recuperate from the cramped conditions aboard and to exercise various manoeuvres. The normally quiet Wideawake Airfield for once lived up to its name as the Vulcan bombers and Victor tankers arrived and were ranged on the runway, ready for an attack on Port Stanley.

Air operations at Ascension involved the use of helicopters to redistribute supplies and equipment and troops among the ships, practising heli-borne assaults around the island, air re-supply from the UK and such long-range surveillance as was possible, pending the arrival of the Vulcans and Hercules equipped for in-flight refuelling. The Sea Harriers practised all aspects of their forthcoming role, firing their guns and dropping practice bombs. They also used air-to-ground rockets, as did some of the Wessex and Sea King helicopters. Britain's air power was being finely honed for action.

The forward 4.5-in guns of HMS *Antrim* firing at South Georgia on April 26, seen over two of her Exocet missile canisters. The frigate *Plymouth* ahead of her is also firing her guns.

South Georgia is re-taken

The first sign that the Task Force had got into position for attack came on April 25, when it was revealed that a Sea King helicopter had crashed on the night of Friday April 23, killing a crewman. What was significant was that the Sea King was a troop-carrier, and was probably transferring SAS men from the *Canberra* for a landing on South Georgia. An American newspaper had already claimed that 'two frigates' had left the Task Force south of Ascension and it is now known that the DLG HMS *Antrim* and the frigates *Brilliant* and *Plymouth* had been detached accompanied by the replenishment ship *Tidespring*.

What was not known then was that when the Argentines had captured Grytviken on April 3 the ice-patrol ship HMS *Endurance* had remained close by throughout the landing. She had been sent to the south, and her two Wasp helicopters had been able to watch the invasion without being detected. Although the CO of the *Endurance* had told London that her helicopters would be able to support Lieutenant Keith Mills and his 21 Royal Marines by attacking the Argentines with their AS-12 missiles it was prudently decided by C-in-C Fleet to use the two Wasps to maintain a watch. The ship, formerly the Danish *Anita Dan*, knew the numerous bays and inlets far better than any Argentine navigator, and managed not only to remain undetected for the next three

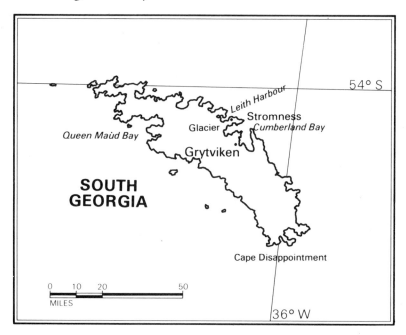

SOUTH GEORGIA

54° S

Leith Harbour
Stromness
Cumberland Bay
Glacier
Queen Maüd Bay
Grytviken

Cape Disappointment

0   10   20   50
MILES

36° W

weeks but also to keep London informed of events at Grytviken.

As early as April 21 a party of 15 men of 22nd SAS had been landed by helicopter on the Fortuna Glacier above Grytviken. It was hoped that they would be able to observe the comings and goings of the Argentine garrison but the weather proved so appalling that they could not operate at all. The winds exceeded 100 mph at times and the temperature was so cold that the party had to ask to be taken off again. Some idea of how grim the conditions were can be guessed from the fact that a Wessex 5 helicopter had to fly in conditions of total 'whiteout' and crashed shortly after takeoff, with the SAS men aboard. A second helicopter arrived, and it too crashed.

News of these incidents was revealed, not through MoD sources, but with the publication in the UK press of a letter written by 18-year-old Leigh Curry, a radio operator on board HMS *Antrim*. In the letter to his father, he told how two Wessexes, one from the RFA *Tidespring*, had crashed on South Georgia three days prior to the landings in a blizzard. Faced with this letter, MoD spokesman, Ian McDonald, admitted the crashes, but stated no announcement had been made for 'operational reasons'. It has since come out that one helicopter crashed while removing the detachment of SAS. A second Wessex coming to take them out also crashed, and it was left to a Wessex HAS.3 from HMS *Antrim*, flown by Lt-Cdr Ian Stanley to take out the crews and the special forces.

For this action Lt-Cdr Stanley was awarded the DSO. During the course of two days, according to the citation, he flew seven sorties to rescue the men of the reconnaissance party and the crews of the crashed helicopters. To achieve this he had to fly his helicopter to an area 1800 ft above ground level in snow storms and gale force winds, a feat demanding the highest degree of courage, airmanship and determination.

Undeterred by this near-disaster 15 men of the SAS amphibious troop set off in five Gemini inflatable boats, intent on occupying Grass Island, close to the Argentine positions. The outboard engines of the Gemini craft are notoriously unreliable and lived up to their reputation. One seized almost immediately, allowing the frail craft and its three occupants to be swept away by the gale, and then a second Gemini drifted away. One of them drifted almost beyond the southernmost tip of South Georgia, keeping radio silence in order not to jeopardize the mission, but fortunately the three men were picked up by a helicopter.

Other parties of SAS and the Royal Marines' Special Boat Section got ashore and managed to get into positions from which they could report on movements of the Argentine troops. On Sunday April 27, 30 SAS under the command of Major Guy Sheridan RM came ashore three miles from Grytviken, and by the sheer dash of their attack overran the defences. Only after they had run the Union Flag up the flagpole did a bewildered Argentine officer tell them that they had just run over a minefield.

As the small force of SAS and Marine commandos was getting ready to go ashore two Lynx helicopters from the frigate *Brilliant* were sent in to give support. Close to the harbour they suddenly spotted a submarine running slowly on the surface. It was the 1800-ton *Santa Fé*, (formerly the USS *Catfish*), running reinforcements and supplies to the garrison. The two helicopters immediately started to attack, using machineguns and their short-range AS-12 ground-attack missiles. The submarine made no attempt to submerge, probably because she was in shallow water, but tried to get into Cumberland Bay. There she sank alongside the jetty, with a huge pool of oil spreading astern from holes torn in her fuel tanks by a number of hits.

Before the re-capture of South Georgia, HMS *Endurance* was never far from the scene, and the ship's two Wasps were kept busy on reconnaissance missions and support for the landing. They are also understood to have been involved (probably spotting) with the *Santa Fé* prior to its attack. The Flight Commander of the *Endurance*, Lt-Cdr John Ellerbeck, received the DSC for his part in the operations before and during the repossession of South Georgia. The citation praises the way in which he led his flight 'with great courage, outstanding devotion to duty and conspicuous success'. It went on to say that Lt-Cdr Ellerbeck's flight made several reconnaissance missions and transported troops for the landing on the island. He also took part in the successful attack on the Argentine submarine *Santa Fé*. Many of these sorties were carried out in extreme weather conditions of gale force winds and poor visibility.

At least one of the missions he flew was the landing of a single SAS man at the camp of two film makers, Cindy Buxton and Annie Price, to protect them from any Argentine aggression. On their return to the UK, they showed film of him landing to pick them up, after the repossession, and also of the SAS man instructing the girls how to use a Browning 9-mm automatic pistol.

The fighting ashore lasted about two hours, although Buenos Aires continued to claim that bloody fighting was continuing as the Royal Marines were 'hunted down' by the garrison. For some reason the destroyer *Exeter* was believed to have been the major British unit present, and she was claimed to have been damaged; in fact none of the four British ships in the area was damaged.

It was at this point that Rear Admiral Woodward made a statement which was to cause some concern at home. Talking on board the flagship he said, 'South Georgia was the appetizer. Now this is the heavy punch coming up behind. My battle group is properly formed and ready to strike. This is the run up to the big match which in my view should be a walk-over'. It struck a confident note but clearly the overtones of arrogance, not to say complacency, caused concern in London, and only 24 hours later the Admiral changed his tune, saying that any assault on the Falklands was bound to be a bloody affair, a forecast much closer to reality.

Tightening the net

Events now began to move more rapidly; on April 28 the British Government announced a Total Exclusion Zone around the Falklands, to take effect from noon on April 30. The terms excluded not only warships and naval auxiliaries but all military and civil aircraft and any Argentine merchant ships. This gave the British the right to treat any ship or aircraft found in the area as hostile, in particular any vessels or aircraft already in the islands.

On Saturday May 1, just one month after the Argentine invasion, the British launched a dramatic air raid on the Port Stanley airport, using a solitary Vulcan bomber flying from Ascension. Wideawake Airfield was the forward base of Vulcan XM607 of 101 Sqn, when in company with a back-up Vulcan and a Victor tanker support, it flew off on its raid on April 30, 1982. It is now known that 19 Victor tanker sorties were required to mount this one raid. It arrived over its target at 4.40 am on May 1 (Admiral 'Sandy' Woodward's birthday) and dropped a mix of 21 1000-lb high explosive and delayed action bombs across the runway. Only one bomb actually hit the runway, but those that fell either side inflicted considerable damage to fuel and ammunition dumps, as well as damaging aircraft on the ground. The biggest casualty, however, was Argentine pride.

The official UK MoD statement on the raid by 'Vulcan aircraft operating from Ascension and refuelled in the air by

The conning tower of the submarine *Santa Fe* (*above left*), which was forced aground at Grytviken after being attacked by two Lynx helicopters from HMS *Brilliant*. Most of her crew and the 40 soldiers aboard surrendered but subsequently one crewman, who had remained in hiding, was shot by Royal Marines. The ice-patrol ship HMS *Endurance* (*below left*), also helped in the attack and played a vital role in reporting the Argentine invasion three weeks earlier. In the background is HMS *Plymouth*.

Victor tankers' did no justice to the remarkable feat of airmanship involved. The aircraft, with one probable back-up aircraft made the longest raid in RAF history. The 7000-mile round trip took some 15 hours, and was refuelled by Victor K.2 tankers of 55 and 57 Sqns. It is interesting to note that the underside paint scheme of light aircraft grey had been overpainted in dark sea grey to render the bat-like silhouette of the Vulcan less susceptible to observation in the pre-dawn half-light over Port Stanley.

The effect of this raid (and the subsequent Sea Harrier attack on the airfield) was to provoke the Argentines into making a propaganda success of the British losses in the air (sic); but they were right about one thing: the runway had not been taken out of action. Damaged it was, but still usable by aircraft with short takeoff and landing (STOL) capabilities like the C-130 Hercules. If the airfield was to be put out of action, then further raids would have to be made. The next raid came on May 4 when another one (possibly two) Vulcans paid a return visit to Port Stanley airfield. Both these raids were followed up by Sea Harriers, also hitting the smaller grass airstrip at Goose Green, before returning to the *Hermes* about 90 miles away.

The Sea Harriers were armed with their twin 30-mm Aden cannon, plus three bombs, either 1000-lb conventional high explosive bombs or BL755 cluster weapons; and later the RAF Harrier GR.3s were to use the Paveway laser-guided bombs. The attacks involved dropping the bombs on (usually) pre-determined targets, and general ground strafing with cannon at targets of opportunity.

The Argentine response was to 'hosepipe' the sky with light anti-aircraft fire. Despite the intensity of this 'Triple-A' (AAA means anti-aircraft artillery in air force jargon) only one Sea Harrier was damaged in the first raid on May 1—by a single bullet in its rudder. It is interesting to note that the only losses to enemy action were from ground fire. It is thought that neither the British-supplied Tigercat nor the French-supplied Roland surface-to-air missiles (SAMs) known to be deployed in defence of the area were brought into action by the Argentines on the initial raids. It is reported (but unconfirmed) that Roland was responsible for downing one RAF Harrier GR.3 later in the conflict. An Argentine Blowpipe (also British-supplied) was responsible for shooting down an RAF Harrier later in the conflict.

A Vulcan bomber takes off from RAF Waddington in Lincolnshire in April (*above left*), before heading for Ascension. The Vulcans were fitted with wing pylons to carry either Sidewinder missiles for self-defence or Shrike anti-radiation missiles. They bombed Port Stanley airfield (*below*). This photograph was taken after the first raid; the oblique line of 1000-lb bomb hits is visible, but contrary to official reports they failed to put the runway out of action. The bombs were intentionally dropped across the runway to ensure at least one hit.

Two frames from a Sea Harrier's gun camera. (*Left*) A Sidewinder missile has just fired. (*Right*) The missile explodes as it homes on to an Argentine Mirage.

There was a lull during the day, but around 5.50 pm the Argentine Air Force tried to attack the Task Force, sending in a force of Dagger fighter-bombers. This attack was met by Sea Harriers of the Combat Air Patrol (CAP), and a Sidewinder heat-seeking missile brought down one Mirage. A second attacker tried to avoid the Sea Harriers by flying through the barrage of fire from the Port Stanley defences, and was brought down, almost certainly an 'own goal' by an Argentine gunner. A further attack by Canberra bombers was even more roughly handled by the *Invincible*'s CAP, one being shot down and the other damaged. The escorting frigate HMS *Arrow* was hit by splinters which wounded one sailor.

The pilot of the Sea Harrier was an RAF officer seconded to the Fleet Air Arm on an exchange tour of duty, Flt Lt Bertie Penfold, flying from the *Hermes*. He described how he shot down the Dagger, after it had fired a missile at another Sea Harrier.

'The Harrier accompanying me broke away from the missiles and I was able to turn up and into the enemy. I locked a Sidewinder into his jet wake and after three or four seconds the missile hit. There was an enormous explosion and I felt quite sick. Being a pilot myself it was sad to see an aircraft explode. But it's got to be done.'

The first round had clearly gone to the British; the Task Force had got into position and had not been deterred or chased away by two air attacks. Although the enthusiastic claims that Port Stanley airport had been put out of action proved premature the noose of the blockage was now around the neck of the garrison and could be tightened at leisure.

The *Belgrano* sinks

Nothing had been heard of the *Armada Republica Argentina*, but on Sunday May 2, at about 2.00 am the British nuclear submarine

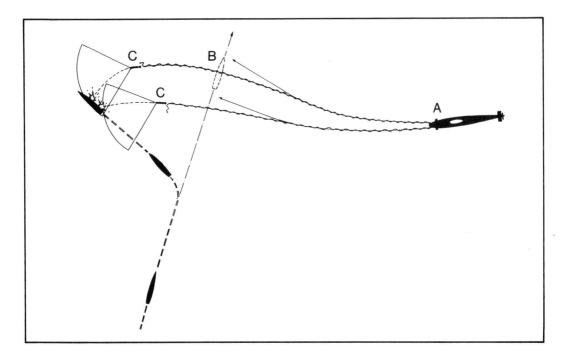

How a submarine would attack a surface warship using two Tigerfish wire-guided torpedoes. From the moment of firing (A) the torpedoes are steered by signals down a fine two-channel wire paying out from spools in the tube and in the torpedo itself. If the vessel turns away from its estimated course (B) the torpedoes are steered on a new interception course, and when they are close to the target (C) the acoustic homing head switches to active tracking and the motor changes to high speed. Initially, it was thought that this was the way in which the *Belgrano* was sunk.

Conqueror detected a large ship on her sonar. The hunter-killer submarine was patrolling an estimated 36 miles outside the Total Exclusion Zoné, and her quarry was the 44-year-old cruiser *General Belgrano*, escorted by two destroyers. Exactly what this elderly ship was doing in such an exposed position was never explained but we do know that Admiral Woodward had sent two of his frigates to the south side of the Falklands to prevent ships from breaking the blockade or from getting through to South Georgia. We also know that the *General Belgrano*'s triple 6-in guns were trained to starboard and were elevated, indicating that she was about to begin a gun-action.

Whatever his orders or intentions Captain Bonzo was never to be given the chance to carry them out, for at about 2.00 am a Mk 8 non-guided torpedo ripped into the cruiser's hull. It was thought originally that two Mk 24 Tigerfish had been used, but it has now been confirmed that the older Mk 8 was despatched. The Tigerfish, it was feared, was unsuitable for sinking a surface vessel.

The *General Belgrano* might still have made it back to port, and Captain Bonzo is even reported to have signalled that he had only lost steering, but his escorting destroyers chose not to offer any help. Nor can it be said that they preferred to hunt for the submarine, for HMS *Conqueror*'s CO, Commander Christopher Wreford-Brown, later reported that neither escort had made any attempt to carry out a sonar search.

When HMS *Conqueror* returned to Faslane on July 3 Commander Wreford-Brown confirmed that the submarine had been shadowing her quarry for some days, and that permission to carry out the attack had come from the C-in-C Fleet at Northwood. It was also confirmed that the *Conqueror* had been at sea for 90 days, nearly a month longer than any previous underwater cruise by a British nuclear submarine. He said that the *General Belgrano* had been judged to be a threat to ships of the Task Force, and pointed out that her escorts were armed with Exocet missiles.

The crippled cruiser was left to wallow in a rising sea. Good damage control training might have enabled her crew to stem the flooding but as every hour went by the ship sank lower in the water. Late the next day the Argentine Joint Services Head-quarters announced that the cruiser was presumed to have sunk south-east of Los Estadar Island, and newspapers speculated that as many as 800 of her crew had drowned. Mercifully the death-toll came down to about 350 as rescue craft and planes located numerous inflatable rafts and boats, but nobody could doubt that the shooting war had begun.

Some eight hours after the torpedoeing of the *General Belgrano* two armed tugs, the *Alferez Sobral* and *Comodoro Somellera* were searching for survivors when they sighted a Sea King helicopter from the *Hermes*. The two patrol craft were about 90 miles inside the Exclusion Zone, and when they unwisely fired on the heli-copter with heavy machine guns the pilot called up two Lynx helicopters from nearby frigates to deal with the interlopers. The Lynxes were armed with the new Sea Skua anti-ship missile, and hits from these sank the *Comodoro Somellera* and severely damaged the *Alferez Sobral*.

The Argentines now seemed as determined to defy the blockade as the British were to enforce it. Diplomatic negotia-tions had proved fruitless, and both sides were now committed to the use of force. Just what that meant would soon become frighteningly clear.

Chapter 4
The Sheffield Sinks

I t was Tuesday May 4 and the British Task Force was ploughing through a comparatively calm sea north of the Falklands. About 20 miles ahead of the flagship was HMS *Sheffield*, a 3500-ton destroyer armed with Sea Dart air-defence missiles. In addition to defending the Fleet with her missiles the *Sheffield*'s task was to act as a 'radar picket', using her big Type 966 'bedstead' radar to detect hostile ships and aircraft, giving the flagship timely warning of hostile activity and enabling the Admiral to take counteraction.

It was shortly before noon, always referred to in the Royal Navy as the 'dinner hour', and the ship was at Defence Stations, the second state of readiness. This was to allow the 270 officers and ratings to share six-hour watches, resting from the gruelling routine of being closed up at Action Stations, eating a meal or simply getting some sleep.

The Captain, 42-year-old James 'Sam' Salt was on the bridge, and a message was apparently being transmitted to Fleet HQ at Northwood on the satellite communications link. The amount of electro-magnetic energy generated by the Type 966 air warning radar (outwardly similar to Type 965) interferes with the satellite transmissions, and to prevent this the radar set had to be shut down. This did not mean, however, that the *Sheffield* was robbed of radar cover, for the flagship *Hermes* was providing her with a radar picture by means of a data-link.

What followed next has to be reconstructed from snippets of information gleaned from highly reliable but unofficial sources,

Men muster on the forecastle of the *Sheffield*, clear of the dense clouds of smoke from burning fuel and cabling. Soon the decks would be too hot to walk on.

The theory of point-defence and area defence for a task force. The carrier in the centre of the formation (A) protects herself with pointdefence Seawolf missiles or guns, while the Sea Dart missile-armed destroyers (B) provide an 'umbrella' over the whole task force. Anti-submarine frigates (C) ahead and astern are provided with point-defence in case they become detached from the main formation.

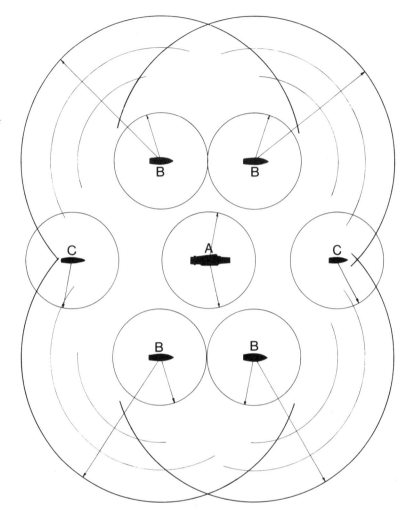

but until such time as the results of the official enquiry is made public (which could be in the year 2012) little can be said. In the Operations Room a suspicious reading was seen on the central Action Information Organization (AIO) plot. Three aircraft targets were identified, but when they were seen to turn away it was assumed that they were merely testing the Task Force's defences and were either declining to attack or were looking for another angle of attack.

Then the Electronic Support Measures (ESM) equipment began to flash a warning that a search radar had locked on to the ship. There was apparently some delay in comprehending the significance of this ESM reading, and by the time the 'PeeWo' (PWO or Principal Warfare Officer) realized that it was a missile's homing head there was only time to shout 'Take cover' to everyone in the Ops Room. Captain Salt himself saw the orange glow of the Exocet's rocket motor and a trail of smoke. In his own words, there was only four or five seconds' warning before a massive explosion shook the ship and plunged it into darkness.

The 'terror' weapon

The *Sheffield* had been hit on the starboard side amidships at about the level of No 2 Deck (one deck below the weather deck) by an air-launched guided missile. Known as the AM-39 Exocet, it was manufactured in France by Societé Nationale Industrielle et Aérospatiale, known usually as Aérospatiale. It was first introduced about ten years ago, as a ship-launched missile known as MM-38, and was subsequently adapted in a lighter version for launching from aircraft. Its chief virtue is that it is a fire and forget missile, which can be pre-programmed to fly in the direction of the target. About two-thirds the way towards the target it descends to within as little as 23 ft above the water, and a radar homing device in the nose-cone switches itself on.

A sea-skimming missile like Exocet is a lethal weapon; its small cross-section is hard to detect with older long waveband radars, particularly during its final run, and the homing head does not begin to emit pulses until it is comparatively close. There are ways of defeating a sea-skimmer but they rely on ultra-rapid electronic analysis of the pulses from the homing head; it can then be jammed or decoyed by means of clouds of chaff (metallic strips cut to reflect an echo resembling a much bigger target) fired from rockets. The main defence against such missiles must always be to prevent them from hitting the ship, either by shooting down the aircraft before it can launch the missile, by shooting down the missile itself or by defeating its homing head.

With the luckless *Sheffield* none of these things happened. The 364 lb warhead smashed through the thin steel plating at a fine angle and passed into the forward engine room, travelling aft. Incredibly, one badly burned survivor remembered seeing the missile tear through the ship's side and pass over the main casing of the gas turbines. It has now been confirmed that the warhead did not detonate, and the damage visible in photographs confirms this. The survivors did report hearing a massive explosion but this would have been the impact of 1455 lb of missile body striking the hull. The results were catastrophic.

The friction as the Exocet passed through the thin steel

'The *Sheffield* ablaze after being hit by an Exocet missile on May 4. The frigate *Arrow* stands by playing her fire hoses on the white-hot steel (*above right*), while a Sea King hovers overhead. One reason why *Sheffield* casualties were relatively low compared with the *Belgrano* was that support ships came in very close to her, whereas the *Belgrano*'s escorts sailed away quickly. The *Belgrano* also perished in a heavy swell, and attempts to tie life rafts together were thwarted. The Exocet holed the *Sheffield* below the waterline and penetrated the engine room, travelling aft. The vertical stripe from the funnel-top to the waterline (*below right*) is an experimental method of reducing the infrared signature, and is not a recognition stripe.

plating of the hull caused a sheet of flame, and this coupled with unspent solid fuel, started a fire which set the main fuel supply tanks on fire. The Royal Navy uses diezo, a light distillate fuel which is considerably safer than the normal aviation fuel used in gas turbines, but at such temperatures it was bound to ignite, and within seconds a column of dense white smoke rose above the ship.

Worse was to follow, as the fierce heat set alight to PVC covering of cables, foam rubber mattresses and other inflammable materials, generating thick black clouds of toxic smoke. Contrary to what has been said in some newspapers, the missile did not impact in the Mechanical Control Room, the nerve-centre of the ship, but the fire started a deck below and generated toxic fumes, including chlorine and possibly phosgene, which asphyxiated the men manning the Mechanical Control Room. These very brave men had in fact remained at their posts in a vain attempt to get power—and pumping-systems—going again. Sadly, they and the cooks in the galley, as well as the men manning the nearby Damage Control Centre were all asphyxiated.

The *Sheffield* and her sisters were designed with four generators, one in each engine room providing main power and two providing standby power. One standby generator was right forward and one was right aft, to avoid the risk of being put out of action by a single hit, but on this occasion all power was lost.

The after main generator was knocked out by the impact of the missile, and the forward one failed a few minutes later. In theory that left two separate power-sources, so why did the ship continue to lack power?

By a tragic coincidence both standby generators were out of action. The forward one was stripped for repair and was waiting for spare parts, while the after generator also proved defective. In any case the initial power failure stopped the ventilation system and permitted the central part of the ship to fill up with dense clouds of smoke.

Fighting the fire

Fire-parties found themselves cut off from both generators, so even if the spares had been available nobody could have reached the generators to get them started. To make matters worse an auxiliary gas-turbine-driven fire pump could not be started.

There is much evidence that the scale of personal firefighting equipment was inadequate. The CO_2 foam extinguishers were

quickly used up, and there is no way of changing them on board. Worst of all, however was the lack of breathing apparatus—only five sets were carried

This meant that even the firefighters could not all be equipped to operate in smoke, and as each Survival Support Device (SSD) carries only 10 minutes' air-supply the firefighting effort was limited to five men working for 10 minutes.

There were other hazards as well. Hydraulic equipment such as boat winches, tended to spray highly inflammable hydraulic fluid out of any break in the system. Polyester clothing melted and stuck to the skin, causing hideously complicated burns. In desperation fire-parties were ordered to change into No 6 (tropical) gear; these were made of cotton, which does not melt in contact with intense heat. Nobody who saw the shocked and scorched survivors being helped by medics to the *Hermes* sick-bay can forget the horrific nature of their injuries.

Help was soon on the way for the stricken ship. Helicopters from the *Hermes* and other ships carried across portable pumps and fire-hoses, while the frigate *Arrow* went alongside to provide firefighting parties. But all efforts were defeated by the smoke. Even with extra breathing apparatus and pumps the fire-parties were blind, and could not get to the heart of the fire or reach injured men. The narrow passageways and small compartments of a warship are a firefighter's nightmare, and it is no discredit to the parties from the various ships of the Task Force and from *Sheffield* herself that after five hours Captain Salt gave the order to 'Abandon Ship'. He told afterwards how the steel decks of his once-proud command became so hot that his shoes began to burn through the soles. In places the plating was white-hot, and the heat was passing down the hull, starting fires elsewhere in cabling. There was also the growing risk of the fire reaching the magazines forward, containing not only 22 Sea Dart missiles (the ship had not had time to load or fire any Sea Darts) but about 120 rounds of 4.5-in shells in the forepart of the ship; aft there were also anti-submarine torpedoes and chaff-rockets likely to explode and cause further casualties.

The ship is scuttled

It was a sad but inevitable decision, but surprisingly the gutted hulk that had been HMS *Sheffield* remained afloat. The salvage tug *Irishman* was ordered to take her in tow, for Admiral Woodward had been told by London that if possible the Navy's technical

A badly burned survivor from the *Sheffield* is helped to the sick-bay by medical orderlies aboard the flagship *Hermes*. Fortunately the weather was calm and helicopters were able to evacuate the injured rapidly.

experts would want to examine her to establish just what had caused the fire. But the 'Shiny Sheff' was to have the last word, and it proved impossible to get her to South Georgia.

The weather worsened, and as each wave washed against the 8 ft hole in her side more water found its way below to join the tons of seawater already pumped into the hull by fire-pumps. She sank lower in the water and became more waterlogged. Finally, after five days, the tow was cast off and on May 10 *Sheffield* sank in the South Atlantic deep, hastened on her way by scuttling charges. One point remains to be cleared up. The Sea King helicopters are *reputed* to carry nuclear depth-charges, for attacking deep-diving nuclear submarines. Although there has never been an official admission that a Lynx helicopter (carried on board the *Sheffield*) can also carry this weapon, nor that any nuclear depth-charges were taken south by the Task Force, certain sections of the British press suggested that the destroyer *Sheffield* had to be scuttled because of a radiation hazard.

All that can be said about this at present is that it is far-fetched. Nuclear weapons are not deployed in peacetime exercises for obvious reasons, and the *Sheffield* went straight to the South Atlantic after such exercises. But even if *Sheffield*'s Lynx helicopter

The Exocet anti-ship missile exists in four forms; MM-38 for mounting in ships; AM-39, a lighter version for aircraft; MM-40, a long-range ship-to-ship variant and SM-39, launched by submarines.

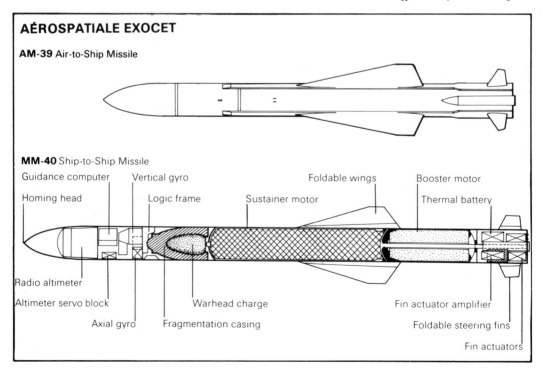

AÉROSPATIALE EXOCET

AM-39 Air-to-Ship Missile

MM-40 Ship-to-Ship Missile

Guidance computer · Vertical gyro · Foldable wings · Booster motor

Homing head · Logic frame · Sustainer motor · Thermal battery

Radio altimeter

Altimeter servo block · Warhead charge · Fin actuator amplifier

Axial gyro · Fragmentation casing · Foldable steering fins

Fin actuators

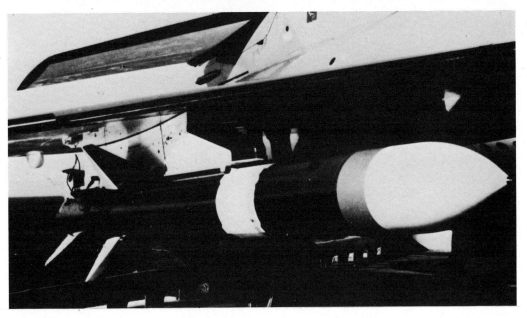

had been equipped to drop a nuclear depth-charge, the outbreak of fire on board would have followed at the earliest opportunity by flooding the magazines. If that had been impossible any dangerous ordnance would have been jettisoned as the next step. What is certain is that firefighters would not have been permitted to remain on board for five hours. The scuttling five days later like that of the trawler *Narwal*, was made necessary because worsening weather had made towing too hazardous.

The AM-39 air-launched version of Exocet mounted under the wing of a French Navy Super Etendard.

How it happened

The attack had been an extremely skilful operation which not only found the weak spot in the Task Force's defences but also showed up a serious lapse by British Naval Intelligence. It was known that the *Armada Republica Argentina* had ordered a total of 14 Super Etendard naval strike aircraft from the well known French firm Avions Marcel Dassault, of which only six had apparently been delivered by the time that the EEC embargo had been imposed.

It was also known that five or six AM-39 Exocets had been delivered by Aérospatiale, but the French Defence Ministry had assured its opposite numbers in London that the French technicians had not started the crucial task of arming the aircraft as the Argentine Navy pilots were still undergoing flying training—the conversion from Skyhawks to their new aircraft.

The fundamental error made by both the French and the British was an assumption that the Argentine Navy personnel would not have sufficient know-how to assemble the Exocets and connect up the complex circuits. Moreover, a team of technicians

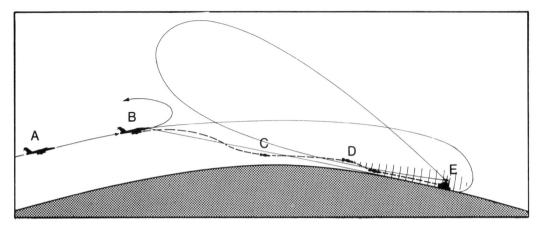

A typical attack using the AM-39 Exocet. When the Super Etendard aircraft (A) gets within range of the target she 'illuminates' it with her Agave radar, feeds the range and bearing into the missile, and fires it, turning away to avoid detection (B). The missile's rocket motor ignites as it descends to its cruise height (C). When five to six miles from the target (D), the radar in the homing head switches itself on and guides the missile to impact.

from Avions Marcel Dassault, the makers of the Super Etendard had been in Argentina since November 1981. It has been alleged that this nine-man team used the test-kit supplied with the missiles to check out the launch pylons and firing circuits aboard the aircraft.

Three faulty circuits were detected and rectified, and then the Super Etendards were ready to fly down to the Comandante Espora Air Base in the south to begin training.

It is also a fact that Argentina is in no way a 'Third World' country; its universities turn out more than enough electronics graduates to provide a high level of technical skill. British electronics firms had already noticed that the Argentine Navy solved the universal problem of maintaining electronics aboard its warships by using officer-technicians rather than junior ratings.

Three hand-picked pilots were chosen to fly the Super Etendards in a strike against the British. It was a risky decision, for a new and untried aircraft with hastily assembled complex weapons could easily develop a fault, but the gamble came off. At about 10.45 on the morning of May 4 the three Super Etendards took off from the Comandante Espora Air Base, a naval air station at the big base at Rio Gallegos, some 470 miles from the Falklands.

To give them sufficient range and more fuel to carry out the attack the aircraft were armed with only one Exocet, allowing them to carry a drop-tank as well. It is not known if the third Super Etendard was carrying an Exocet, as it may have been equipped to refuel the other two, using a special 'buddy pack'.

Little over half an hour after takeoff the three aircraft were within range of the Task Force. They may in fact have been guided towards the British ships by signals from a Neptune maritime patrol aircraft tracking the Task Force on radar.

This theory rests on a report that the flagship *Hermes* sighted a high-level contact on radar. Another explanation, however, is that the third Super Etendard was used to reconnoitre, climbing briefly above the horizon from time to time to obtain a radar-contact.

Once she obtained that vital information about the bearing of the target, all that would be needed would be to pass the figures to his fellow pilots, who could inject them into the fire-control system's computer in each aircraft.

This would have allowed the Super Etendards to approach at low level, not giving away their presence by using their Agave radars. In either case it would have been sufficient merely to obtain the bearing and approximate range of the Task Force from the radar, feed this data into the fire control system aboard the Super Etendard, and then fire the Exocet 'blind'.

The Argentine pilots were reported as saying that they had not fired at any specific ship; radar had detected two 'blips', one large and one smaller, and had fired their Exocets towards these two targets. These targets were presumably the *Sheffield* and the *Hermes*, some 15 or 20 miles beyond.

Two days after the attack on the *Sheffield*, France announced suspension of deliveries of Super Etendards to Argentina. This announcement, coupled with rumours emanating from various 'well informed' sources led to stories in the world's press that as many as 12 to 14 Super Etendards ordered had actually reached Argentina. The truth of the matter has yet to be made public.

Similarly speculation was rife about how many of the Exocet 'terror' weapons had been delivered. The published figure seems to favour five or six (one per aircraft delivered), but again speculation in the press suggested that AM-39 Exocets were being bought on the black market, or that the shipborne version of Exocet, the MM-38 (also in Royal Navy service) was being rapidly converted to an air-launched weapon.

In the case of the first story, there is simply no 'missile-supermarket' at which countries can buy a dozen Exocets off the shelf. The aircraft's weapons system and radar fire control have to be designed and programmed to accept the missile and provide it with information. It is not a bolt-on weapon, and a lot of complex and extensive integration work has to be done to an aircraft before it can accept such a weapon. It is possible, however, that a third country which already possessed the AM-39 might have supplied the missiles. This country would have had to contravene the 'end-use certificate' saying that the missiles would not be passed to another country without the originating country's approval.

The second story, of converting a ship-launched missile, would not be possible at all. Being air-launched, the AM-39 does away with the initial rocket-booster designed to launch the MM-38 from the deck of a ship, and is therefore shorter and lighter. The electronics of the missile would also require much modification. With time and money, it could be done, but not within the period of the Falklands conflict.

The Task Force reaction

Aboard the carrier *Invincible* the sense of helplessness was overwhelming. Her sophisticated command and control equipment gave her a considerably better idea of what was going on than the flagship, whose equipment was much older. On the flag bridge the Commander broadcast a commentary, describing the approach of two aircraft from the west, 'closing . . . 50 miles, 40 miles, 30 miles . . . two missiles have been launched . . . Hit the deck'. Everyone below decks cringed when they heard the roar of rockets, but it was the Corvus chaff-launchers on either side of the funnels, firing their clouds of chaff in the path of a missile. Then came the reassuring announcement that no more missiles were in flight.

The atmosphere aboard *Invincible* changed rapidly thereafter. When the ship had sailed from Portsmouth there was an air of crude jingoistic humour, understandable but taking little account of realities. Only when it was realized that a thousand men might have gone down with the *General Belgrano* did the truth sink in, that a torpedo hitting their own ship might cause a similar death-toll. In fact a submarine attack was later made on the ship, but the torpedo was apparently decoyed by the noisemaker towed astern.

The success of the attack naturally threw the Task Force into confusion. Eyewitnesses testify to the entire mass of ships manoeuvring at high speed. The carrier *Invincible* believed that she was under missile attack, and fired her Corvus chaff-rockets. The Super Etendards had fired only two Exocets (indicating that the third aircraft was possibly on a refuelling mission), but the second missile went nowhere near the *Sheffield*. The frigate *Plymouth* is reported to have decoyed that Exocet by means of chaff.

It was HRH Prince Andrew, serving as a co-pilot in a Sea King crew on board HMS *Invincible* who, inadvertently we assume, revealed the use of helicopters as decoys for the Exocet missiles, following the loss of the *Sheffield*. Sea Kings were ordered, on top of their other duties, to fly ahead and astern of the two carriers dropping chaff in an effort to provide an enlarged radar echo which, it was hoped, would 'spoof' any Exocet launched against the carriers. As far as we know, this ruse proved successful as neither carrier was hit, but further details about these operations are not available.

The loss of the *Sheffield* tended to obscure the fact that the Task Force had not been deflected from its prime objective, the softening up of the Argentine defences ashore. On May 4, Sea Harriers had attacked the runway at Port Stanley, but this time the defenders were better at predicting the attackers' tactics, and one of the Sea Harriers, piloted by Lieutenant Nicholas Taylor RN, was shot down. The 32-year-old Fleet Air Arm pilot was the first British serviceman to be killed in the Falklands conflict, although later that day another 20 men would die in the *Sheffield*.

On Friday May 7 it was announced in London that another two Sea Harriers had been lost, this time through a tragic accident. The weather the day before had been atrocious, with visibility down to 200 yards, and the two Sea Harriers apparently collided. They were being tracked on radar when both echoes

The container ship *Atlantic Conveyor*, in addition to carrying stores between decks, was partially equipped to operate aircraft. Containers were stacked on either side of the deck, to provide shelter from wind and spray. A Sea Harrier is visible landing, with two Chinook and two Wessex helicopters. This photograph was taken when the *Atlantic Conveyor* was still in British waters, and trials were being conducted.

An RAF Harrier at RAF Wittering on April 20. It has just been fitted with Sidewinder missiles to reinforce the Navy's Sea Harriers in the air-defence role. During the conflict, the Harrier pilots profited from having fought mock battles during NATO training exercises against Belgian Mirage aircraft over West Germany, thus learning more about the fighting capabilities of the fighter widely used by Argentina. The exercises were arranged as late as May 17-19.

disappeared and the most likely theory is that the two pilots were suffering from excessive fatigue. Whatever the reason, Lieutenant-Commander Eyton-Jones and Lieutenant Curtis were a tragic loss, being *Invincible's* most experienced pilots.

The loss of three out of 19 Sea Harriers and one-third of the missile-defence around the Task Force inevitably put a much greater strain on operations, but in spite of this the Combat Air Patrol successfully dealt with attempts to beat the blockade; on May 8 a group of Argentine Hercules transports had to turn back and the same happened the following day, even though the transports were escorted by Mirages. An attempt to attack the Task Force was also dealt with, and the Mirages were driven off 50 miles from their targets.

As part of the final encirclement of the Falklands before the invasion the British extended their Total Exclusion Zone to within 12 miles of the Argentine coast. This extension, which came into force on Friday May 7, gave British submarines greater freedom to operate close to the three main naval bases and to 'bottle up' the Argentine Navy. In retrospect this policy worked far better than had been expected, for no movements of surface warships were reported subsequently, and even the threat of submarine attack did not materialize. Shortly after the attack on the *Sheffield* there had been a submarine alarm and ships and helicopters had carried out a counter-attack, but subsequently the contact was announced to be 'non-submarine'. However a rumour persisted that *Sheffield* had been attacked by torpedoes.

Several more warships had already been despatched to the South Atlantic, including at least one more Type 42 destroyer armed with Sea Dart missiles, but the most welcome reinforcement was a force of 14 Harriers and 8 Sea Harriers, which arrived on May 8. These had flown non-stop from Yeovilton Naval Air Station in Somerset down to Ascension, a distance of about 3500 miles with RAF Victor tanker support. Some 809 Sqn Sea Harriers were turned round swiftly and air-refuelled down to the Task Force, and the remainder were loaded aboard the transport SS *Atlantic Conveyor*, bound for the Task Force.

Some idea of the scale of the build-up of supplies and men was given by an official announcement on Monday May 10, to the effect that a zone of controlled airspace had been declared within a 100-mile radius of Wideawake Airfield on Ascension Island. The purpose of this declaration was not for security reasons, but to prevent accidents.

The air and sea blockade of the Falklands was difficult to maintain with such slender forces, and throughout this period light transports and small ships slipped in and out. Not all were successful, however, and early on the morning of Sunday May 9 two Sea Harriers spotted what appeared to be a fishing trawler.

She was in fact the *Narwal*, a requisitioned Argentine fishing vessel which had been shadowing the Task Force for some days. As she was well within the TEZ she was a legitimate target in any case, and the aircraft opened fire with their 30-mm Aden guns and dropped a small bomb. The crew, having lost one dead and 13 injured out of 25 immediately abandoned ship, and when a Sea King arrived to board the *Narwal* it was discovered that she had been under naval command and was fitted with surveillance gear for monitoring British movements. Her career as a Royal Navy prize was short-lived, however, for the following day the same gale which put an end to the agony of *Sheffield* made it impossible to get the *Narwal* to South Georgia. She too was cast off and allowed to sink.

What might be termed Round 1 of the Falklands Crisis was now over. The score was a grim one, nearly 400 men dead and at least four ships sunk, all within a week. It must not be forgotten that all the while frantic diplomatic activity had been in progress. But all that remained certain was that neither Argentina nor Britain could negotiate without being accused of betraying the men who had died.

Chapter 5
Battle for the Falklands

The first sign that the Task Force was moving in much closer than before came early on the morning of Tuesday May 11. The night before the frigate *Alacrity* had made a daring run through Falkland Sound, the 60-mile long passage which separates East Falkland from West Falkland. The frigate steamed fast, without lights, twisting and turning to keep in the channel.

Close to Port Howard, a small harbour on the north-eastern side of West Falkland, the search radar picked out a target, 'bigger than the *Narwal* but smaller than a frigate', and she immediately opened fire with her 4.5-in gun. Although British reports talked of a big explosion and the general assumption was that the mystery ship had been sunk, this was denied by Argentine official sources. She was the mercantile vessel *Isla de Estados*, a small cargo carrier, probably pressed into service to run fuel, ammunition and food through the blockade.

Clearly the British military leaders were not prepared to risk a headlong assault on the islands, and a more cautious approach called for the greatest number of troops. Taken literally this could have meant that nothing would happen until the liner *Queen Elizabeth II* arrived with the 3000 men of 5 Infantry Brigade.

Preparing for invasion

Although the Task Force was not yet ready to begin the amphibious landings it remained fully engaged. On the same day that the *QE2* sailed the frigate HMS *Brilliant* shot down two A-4 Skyhawk fighter-bombers trying to attack the Task Force in

A *Rothesay* class frigate, probably HMS *Plymouth*, wreathed in smoke as she fires her Seacat missiles at a Mirage III passing overhead during prolonged Argentine attacks in San Carlos Water. British warships were extremely fortunate that the Argentines fuzed the majority of bombs wrongly so that many failed to explode or exploded at the wrong time.

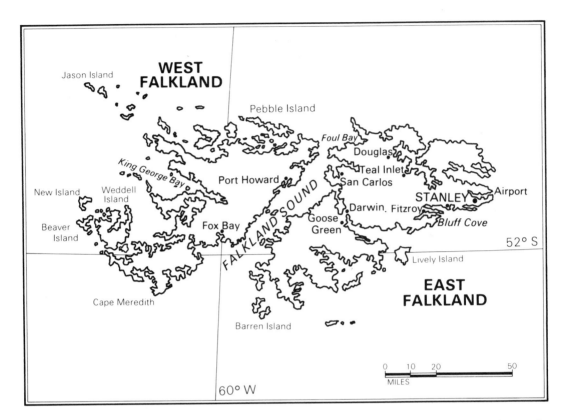

Falkland Sound. The small Seawolf missile was the Royal Navy's newest anti-aircraft weapon, with the added capability of being able to shoot down missiles (on occasion it even shot down stray British missiles!). Its main characteristic is automatic response to any threat, particularly at low level. Some weeks later the film of this engagement was shown on television, showing just how rapidly the Type 910 tracker radar and its TV camera lock on to the target. The attacks on May 12 accounted for three Skyhawks, for a third aircraft while frantically trying to avoid a Seawolf, spun out of control into the sea.

The Argentine defenders, reckoned to number about 9000 men (subsequently it was learned that more than 11 000 had landed since April 2) had clearly dispersed their aircraft around the islands. The ravaged airfield at Port Stanley was too obvious a target, and most of the valuable Pucará ground attack aircraft were dispersed to outlying airstrips.

One of these was Pebble Island, just north of West Falkland and close to the entrance to Falkland Sound. During the night of Friday May 14 a force of SAS attacked Pebble Island and destroyed 11 Pucarás, ammunition and fuel. To hide the fact that SAS were involved the action was reported to have involved only Royal Marine Commandos, while further camouflage was provided by a heavy bombardment of Port Stanley.

The BBC's reporter Brian Hanrahan told in his despatch how a Royal Artillery Forward Observation Officer calmly relayed instructions to the frigates and destroyers supporting the SAS at Pebble Island. Orange cordite flash lit up the night repeatedly, interspersed with the blinding white glare of starshell, used to illuminate the Argentine ground positions.

The purpose of the Pebble Island raid was to reduce the chance of the Pucará aircraft harassing any landing in the area, and of course, to continue the harassment of the whole Argentine force. The nightly raids, coupled with the fear, justified or not, that SAS units were already ashore, was slowly wearing down the morale of the defenders.

One of the reporters with the Task Force described the last-minute preparations for the landing, in a despatch filed on May 20, just 24 hours before it began. He described flying over the *Canberra* and seeing her floodlit decks, while helicopters 'cross-decked' her troops to the assault ships and landing craft which would carry out the landings. Despite the risk, floodlighting facilitated the transfer of troops, and as she was out of range of air strikes there was no risk of attack from Mirages, only from submarines.

The carriers were also being brought up to strength, with Harriers and Sea Harriers moving across from the deck of the *Atlantic Conveyor*. The aircraft were packed so tightly aboard the 18 000-ton ship that they had to take off vertically before flying off to join the carriers.

During these cross-decking operations the SAS sustained the worst casualties in the regiment's history. A Sea King HC.4 helicopter carrying 30 men crashed into the sea, killing all 21 SAS men on board. The helicopter was first thought to have been hit by part of the ship's superstructure as she lifted off the deck, but subsequently it was announced that a large seabird such as an albatross had probably flown into the tail-rotor.

A helicopter hovering or taking off at slow speed is at her most vulnerable, and without the directional stability given by the tail-rotor the pilot can easily lose control. In theory there is a chance to get out of the narrow fuselage, but from personal experience I can say that the chances are remote, given the bulky packs and life-preservers which everyone would be wearing.

An amphibious landing is the most risky of all naval operations, as history has shown. The naval force has to linger off a beach, exposed to air attack, while the troops are vulnerable to counter-attacks in the first few hours of getting ashore. The classic defence against an amphibious landing is to hit the attackers before they can establish their bridgehead ashore. If a secure footing is not achieved the result easily becomes a bloody fiasco, with ships sustaining heavy casualties as they try to evacuate the surviving troops under fire. It was a nightmare which must have troubled not only Admiral Woodward and the Land Commander, General Moore, but also the Service Chiefs back in London.

The attack begins

For the defenders the first sign that the long-awaited landing was about to start came at about 8.30 am (local time) on May 21 when Argentine lookouts at the small harbour of Port San Carlos, on the north-western side of East Falkland saw ships moving into San Carlos Water. Shells began to fall on the defensive positions, and within half an hour the first wave of troops was safely ashore. They were guided ashore by parties of SAS who had reconnoitred the Argentine positions, and had provided the Task Force commanders with the confirmation that the San Carlos area was lightly defended.

Surprise appeared to be complete, but radio-messages had already gone out to the Port Stanley garrison. Within minutes of the first reports air strikes were being prepared from Rio Gallegos, while the Pucarás prepared to strafe ground positions.

The air-sea battle which ensued was bitter and bloody as the Mirages and Skyhawks came over in massive numbers, as many as 72 aircraft on the first day. The Combat Air Patrol of Sea Harriers valiantly intercepted the attackers and inflicted heavy casualties, but the odds were too heavy and before long aircraft began to 'leak' through the defences, getting through to the packed mass of ships lying in San Carlos Water.

The Argentine Air Force flew most of these air strikes, the bulk of them being flown by the Mirage IIIEAs, Daggers and Skyhawks in the sort of strength which allowed the Sea Harriers and naval SAMs, and later the ground-based Rapier SAMs to take their toll of the intruders, while still leaving some aircraft over the target to drop their bombs. The stock of bombs used by the Argentines must have left something to be desired, as many failed to explode either on contact with the water or after hitting ships.

It also became clear that many of the aircrew involved on the Argentine side were not long out of their operational training, but what they lacked in experience they made up for in courage and determination. Later in the conflict, the ground attack Pucarás and even Aermacchi MB.339 trainers were used against the Fleet. Indeed, it was rockets from an MB.339 which hit the *Ardent*, causing her eventual loss (no fewer than 14 rockets ripped open her port side). The supplies of napalm discovered at Goose Green were probably destined to be delivered by the Pucarás and MB.339s, and it is fortunate that this terrible anti-personnel weapon was never actually used in the conflict.

The Battle of 'Bomb Alley'
The air attacks did not go unpunished. The destroyers hit back with Sea Dart missiles, the frigates used their short-range Seacat missiles, and once the Army had got its Rapier missile batteries set up ashore it was possible to put up a fearsome barrage of fire across the bay. Ground troops also used their Blowpipe hand-held missiles to protect themselves from the Pucará close-

Pucarás and helicopters were dealt with by Blowpipe shoulder-launched missiles. Ironically, the British-made missile was also used effectively by the Argentine forces on the islands.

A Seawolf missile leaving the launcher. More up-to-date than the Seacat, the Seawolf was unfortunately absent from the majority of British warships. The question which must be answered is why. The Seawolf's first use in action by HMS *Brilliant* accounted for three Skyhawks.

support aircraft which soon arrived from local airstrips such as Goose Green.

The frigate *Brilliant* had been the first British warship to shoot down an Argentine aircraft, when her Seawolf missiles destroyed three Skyhawks on May 12. In Falkland Sound she proved her capabilities as a command ship by directing the *Invincible*'s Sea Harriers against the incoming waves of attackers, and her First Lieutenant, Lt-Cdr Lee Hulme reported later that the ship's plotting facilities had helped the Sea Harriers to shoot down a claimed 7 Mirages and 5 Skyhawks.

The *Brilliant* lived up to her name, and her luck held out to the end. Even when three bombs dropped nearby they bounced off the water, rising higher than the superstructure and the masthead. Later when splinters sliced through the power-cables of one of the Seawolf launchers, Marconi technicians aboard were able to rig up an emergency cable *outside* the hull. This jury-rig may not have been in the rules but it kept the vital Seawolf system working, the only defence that the Task Force had against Exocets.

There was no hope for the *Ardent*, which sank towards nightfall with the loss of 22 men dead, but her sister *Antelope* did not at first appear to be badly damaged. The civilian NAAFI canteen manager organized five soldiers in a desperate defence with their GPMG light machine guns. (Although such a defence had never-been envisaged against modern aircraft several ships, including the *Canberra*, organized troops into extemporized AA teams.) One bomb had hit the *Antelope*'s stern, starting a fire, while another lodged in her engine room without exploding. The captain, Commander Nicholas Tobin, took his injured ship gingerly down San Carlos Water to a sheltered anchorage, where she could drop anchor and give her damage control parties a chance to save her.

For hours a bomb disposal expert, Staff Sergeant Jim Prescott of the Royal Engineers, worked in the engine room, trying to save the ship, but during the night it exploded, killing him and a naval rating. The blast set the *Antelope* ablaze, and horrified onlookers watched her burn to the waterline. A dense cloud of smoke hung over her like a funeral pall, and eventually an explosion broke her back. The bow and stern remained sticking out of the water after her fires were finally extinguished .

Other ships were hit by bombs but mercifully none of them exploded. The frigate *Argonaut* was hit by one bomb which passed through the plating below the waterline. It penetrated a fuel tank and wrecked the Seacat missile magazine. Two sailors manning the hoist to the missile-launcher above, Able Seaman Boldy and Stoker Stuart were killed, and for a horrible moment it looked as if the magazine might explode. In the opinion of Captain Layman, what saved the ship was an inrush of fuel oil and seawater; it put the fires out before the Seacat warheads could be 'cooked off'. One of her two boilers was wrecked but this did not prevent her from firing her guns and missiles.

A typical Sea Dart Surface-to-Air Missile (SAM) engagement: the target-indicating Type 992Q radar (A) at the masthead identifies an incoming hostile aircraft, and designates it to the Type 909 tracker radar (B). The tracker 'illuminates' the target and the missile-launcher (C) fires a Sea Dart. The booster falls clear (D), while the missile climbs towards the target, until its warhead acquires energy reflected from the target (E), and steers itself to impact (F).

A bomb falls astern of the frigate *Argonaut* in San Carlos Water on May 25. Two men died when one bomb went into her magazine and another destroyed a boiler, but the ship managed to remain operational. The defence of 'Bomb Alley' was a time of frustration for Sea Harrier pilots. Deprived of airborne early warning, they had the unsuitable task of acting as an outer cordon in the defence screen. They shot down many aircraft but some got through with disastrous results.

Another ship which had a very lucky escape was the 'County' class DLG *Antrim*, which had a large bomb in her after engine room. A bomb disposal expert managed to defuze it safely, and temporary patches were welded over the holes. One bomb hit the frigate *Broadsword*, passed through the hull and continued on an *upward* trajectory. Even so, it still failed to burst when it hit the water beyond the ship. It was widely believed that the Argentine armourers had set the bombs' fuzes to be dropped from a greater height, and had failed to allow for the suicidally low runs made by their pilots. However some aviation experts blame the tendency of countries like Argentina to buy 'cheap and nasty' bombs on the international market, and to use inferior fuzes.

The ferocity of Argentine attacks came as an unpleasant shock to everyone in the Task Force, for it had been fondly imagined, not only in the Royal Navy, that the developments in defensive missile weaponry had made such close-range air attacks impossible. What was happening, in fact, was that missiles were proving extremely deadly, so much so that they created what amounted to 'zones of lethality'. Unfortunately, like all weapons, missiles have arcs and altitudes at which they are ineffective, and the attacking aircraft were quick to find these blind spots.

British warships had been armed to fight a NATO war in the North Atlantic, and it has long been NATO doctrine to ignore the risk from shore-based air attack. The only close-range armament carried in British warships is the Seacat missile, the 20-mm Oerlikon gun and the 40-mm Bofors gun, both of the guns being veterans of the Second World War. The Seacat-armed ships had at least a fighting chance of hitting an aircraft, for at low altitude the aircraft could not use its maximum speed, and even the 20-mm and 40-mm guns proved capable of inflicting damage, but these guns had no fire control.

The Type 42 destroyers were not even given the Seacat missile system as they were too small, a grievously short-sighted economy. The only ships which held their own in all these attacks were the Seawolf-armed ships *Broadsword* and *Brilliant*, and it was noticeable that the more experienced Argentine pilots gave them a wide berth when they recognized them.

The Argentine pilots were paying a bloody price for their success, however. By midnight on May 24 British official estimates of the losses were as follows:

21 Mirages/Daggers shot down (leaving an estimated 23)
 1 Canberra shot down (leaving 8)
13 Skyhawks shot down (leaving an estimated 63)
 2 Pucarás shot down, 6 destroyed on the ground (leaving an estimated 42)
 2 Puma helicopters shot down, 1 destroyed (leaving 6)
 1 Chinook helicopter destroyed on the ground (leaving 2)
 1 Alouette helicopter shot down, 2 others destroyed (leaving an estimated 50)
 5 unidentified light aircraft destroyed on the ground.

These figures are naturally unreliable, being only British estimates, and there is always an element of double-counting in air warfare. But many experts feel that any inaccuracy in the figures could be balanced by the unknown number of aircraft which failed to get back to Argentina, either because they had been damaged in combat or simply because they ran out of fuel. The distance from home meant that any time spent in combat would drastically reduce the tiny margin of fuel; high-speed evasive manoeuvres use fuel even faster, and low-altitude flying is also expensive.

Argentina redoubles her efforts

The air-attacks reached a new peak on Tuesday May 25, Argentina's Independence Day, when Argentine pilots hurled themselves at the ships with a ferocity which was virtually suicidal. The destroyer *Coventry* stationed to the north of Falkland Sound, where she could give warning of approaching aircraft, was attacked twice. The first wave of Skyhawks was dealt with by firing Sea Dart missiles and shooting down four but a second wave overwhelmed her. Three weeks later her captain, David Hart-Dyke told how the blast of one bomb devastated the Operations Room. The ship capsized shortly afterwards but mercifully casualties were comparatively light with 19 men killed.

The *Coventry* had been given one of the Seawolf-armed frigates, the *Broadsword*, to give her more protection. She was hit by a bomb which destroyed one of her Lynx helicopters and then exited harmlessly through the side plating below the flight deck. Recovering from this near-disaster, her officers and men had time to do no more than watch helplessly as the Skyhawks dealt with the *Coventry* steaming ahead of her.

According to *Broadsword*'s captain, she simply blew up in a sheet of flame and listed sharply to port, blazing furiously. Like the *Sheffield* she was an early Type 42 destroyer; her Type 965/966 and 992Q radars were not ideal for coping with low-level attacks over land, and she had no point-defence.

Much worse was to follow, for the Argentines had decided to use more of their dwindling store of Exocet missiles. The massive container ship *Atlantic Conveyor* was moving into Falkland Sound when she was struck by two Exocets which set her on fire. She had been acting as a spare deck or 'parking lot' for some of the Harriers previously but fortunately the last of these had flown off. However three big Chinook and 12 Wessex HU.5 helicopters were destroyed, with vast quantities of materiél desperately needed by the troops ashore.

Both Exocets had been deflected by chaff fired from HMS *Hermes*, but the missiles' homing heads picked up the nearby target of the merchant ship. In the heat of the moment the *Hermes* probably looked after her own defence without ensuring that the clouds of chaff were placed to protect the *Atlantic Conveyor* as well, which in different circumstances could have been easily done.

No official list has been given of the amount or the nature of the material carried by the ship, but much later it was admitted that some 4500 tents were lost. Much more serious was the destruction of the portable landing strip for the Harriers, and their even more vital refuelling gear. It was subsequently admitted that the loss of all this equipment held up the land campaign by several days.

The *Atlantic Conveyor*'s Master, Captain Ian North, survived the initial blast, for the senior naval officer on board recalls following him down the ladder into the water after 'Abandon Ship' had been ordered. The bitterly cold water apparently killed him, and another three merchant seamen were lost. The 15 000-ton ship had sailed from Devonport on April 25, and all 34 of her crew had volunteered to sail to the Falklands. Her flat upper deck and giant vehicle deck had made her an obvious choice for the Task Force's needs, and she had already played a vital role in the landings.

The maximum effort on May 25 seemed to have exhausted the resources of the Argentine Air Force for there was a lull in the attacks on the ships operating in San Carlos Water. Several attacks were made by Pucará ground-attack aircraft operating from Falklands airstrips (one had been shot down by HMS *Coventry*) and around Port Stanley Puma helicopters were engaged by Harriers. The British claims of aircraft shot down totalled 64 by May 27, and it was claimed that only 50 Skyhawks and Mirages remained operational. Some of these must have been retained to defend mainland targets, for throughout the campaign the Junta in Buenos Aires maintained that the British intended to bomb the airbases.

Breakout from the bridgehead

On Friday May 28 the British, having built up their reserves of ammunition and supplies, made their first move. In a daring attack the 2nd Battalion of the Parachute Regiment, the legendary 'Two Para' moved 25 miles out of the bridgehead and captured the Goose Green and Port Darwin settlements. Apart from the vital airstrip at Goose Green the two settlements on the narrow isthmus connecting the two halves of East Falkland dominate one of the main routes to Port Stanley, and once they were in British hands the advance to Port Stanley could begin.

What made the Goose Green victory outstanding was the disparity of the forces involved. Against all the textbook rules of preponderance of attackers to defenders, 700 paratroopers captured 1400 Argentine soldiers, at a cost of only 12 killed and 31 wounded. Sadly the architect of this astonishing victory, Colonel 'H' Jones was killed during the assault.

There were now 5000 troops ashore, and the ultimate success of the operations was not in doubt. But that should not obscure the difficulties faced by the British throughout this period of the assault. Pooled despatches from journalists with the troops talk of the nightmare of constant air attacks in daylight. The dreaded message on the radio sets, 'Air Raid Red, Air Raid Red, Take Cover Now' started a frantic scramble into muddy trenches.

Television viewers were given a glimpse of the horrors when Surgeon-Commander Rick Jolley revealed that his field hospital had two unexploded bombs in it. The Rapier and Blowpipe batteries added their contribution to the din, screeching

The LSL *Sir Galahad*, just after she had been hit by Argentine bombs in Bluff Cove. The first inflatable life rafts have just been dropped into the water, and the soldiers in the foreground have not yet discarded their weapons. The *Sir Tristram* was also hit and it is claimed that men died because the bow doors refused to open to enable them to disembark as soon as they arrived in Bluff Cove. There may be more sinister reasons. Whatever happened the troops were still on board six hours after arriving in the cove.

away from their launchers as they sought out the Mirages, Skyhawks and Pucarás.

By June 1 the British were on Mount Kent, only 12 miles from Port Stanley, while a second attack to the south had advanced on Fitzroy. This completed the encirclement of the Port Stanley garrison, and left the defenders in the unenviable position of being overlooked from the high ground to the east. The Task Force was less in the news now, but its vital task of supplying the beachhead and providing a Combat Air Patrol continued without respite. At least one attack was made by Argentine aircraft on the ships, but it was shot down by missiles.

A less warlike mission was to evacuate the wounded, both British and Argentine. This was done under the international regulations of the Geneva Convention. On June 2, for example, the 'ambulance ferry' *Hecla*, her hull painted white with a single large red cross arrived at Montevideo. She was flying both British and Uruguayan flags, and had already been boarded and examined by a three-man International Red Cross team. Under the supervision of M Jean-Pierre Givel the 24 Argentine wounded prisoners were examined and questioned to ensure that they had been properly treated, and then they and the 18 British wounded were carried ashore. The Argentines would be taken across the River Plate on board a naval transport but the British were flown home by an RAF VC-10 transport aircraft.

The abiding impression of life aboard the Task Force ships from eyewitness accounts is one of long periods of boredom punctuated with short but very crowded minutes of action. Food tended to be dreary, as Navy cooks lost their peacetime flair in their efforts to cope with meals at odd hours. An officer in the destroyer *Glamorgan* described how official warnings that lack of roughage in the diet would lead to 'loss of regularity and worse disorders' quoted his captain as saying that 'five air raids per day would make roughage superfluous'.

Much surplus equipment had long since been stripped out of the ships. After the fire in HMS *Sheffield* there was little complaint when carpets and chair covers were jettisoned, along with wardroom pianos and sailing dinghies. In the early days Union flags had been painted on forecastles, but otherwise a drab overall grey replaced the normal smart peacetime appearance. Pennant numbers were also painted out, to rob Argentine pilots of any chance of identifying individual frigates and destroyers.

Soldiers and crewmen are shocked and dazed as they reach the shore, with the stricken *Sir Galahad* burning behind them (*above right*), while a Wessex HU.5 winches up a survivor from a life raft.

Disaster at Bluff Cove

On June 9 first news leaked out of what was to prove the worst loss of the campaign. The British had decided that a rapid attack on Bluff Cove, a small harbour on the south-eastern coast, would materially help the drive by the Welsh Guards on Port Stanley. But from the start things went wrong. The Task Force reported that the Sea Harriers could not maintain any cover over such an operation. Brigadier Tony Wilson felt that the risk was still worth taking, and apparently commandeered two logistic landing ships, the Royal Fleet Auxiliaries *Sir Galahad* and *Sir Tristram* to carry companies of Welsh Guards.

The first, *Sir Tristram*, slipped into Bluff Cove on the night of June 7 with Rapier missile batteries and a large supply of ammunition but for reasons not yet explained the second LSL had not started unloading her troops by daylight on June 8, and one report even suggests that they waited six hours in broad daylight before beginning the disembarkation.

It was just the sort of target that the Argentines had been waiting for, and within half an hour the Mirages and Skyhawks were approaching their landfall on the north side of the island. Two Mirages and three Skyhawks swept in low over the bay, raking the ships with rockets and cannon-fire. Two bombs hit *Sir Galahad*, one going through the tank deck and into the accommodation, and the other exploding astern. Her sister *Sir Tristram* was hit by rockets and 20-mm cannon shells which set her on fire.

Sadly the troops were still on board the ships, as the vehicles and Rapier missiles had been sent ashore first, and the casualties among the crowded soldiers were heavy. Men rushed to put on their lifejackets and orange survival suits, while others simply took their chance in the icy water. Burning oil fuel made such attempts suicidal, and it was left to the indefatigable helicopter pilots to plunge into the billowing clouds of smoke and flames.

Although British television viewers were not to see the films of the survivors coming ashore for another three weeks, even after such a delay they brought home the full horror. Fortunately there were many people ashore to pull the badly burned and shocked survivors out of the water as they floundered about. Some of them had been hideously injured by the blast, others were blackened and singed by fire, and some were simply shocked by the rapidity of the catastrophe. Probably the most pathetic survivors were the Hong Kong Chinese civilians who made up the crew of so many Royal Fleet Auxiliaries; like other civilians they had volunteered

for the Falklands with little idea that it would end in such horror.

The disaster at Bluff Cove on June 8 emphasizes the courage and determination shown by the helicopter crews in the rescue role throughout the campaign. 'I vouch it was a day of extraordinary heroism' said ITN reporter Michael Nicholson, who witnessed the event. Let his words tell the story:

'The strong wind fanned the flames—enormous flames—and as the fuel tank exploded, the ship (*Sir Galahad*) was half enveloped in thick black smoke. But the Royal Navy Sea King and Wessex helicopter pilots and their crews ignored the flames. They ignored the explosions and ignored the ammunition erupting around them, and they flew their machines into the smoke to lift the queues of men waiting calmly.

I watched one pilot steer his machine slowly and deliberately into the black smoke and hover. He was completely blinded, completely helpless. I saw his crewman winching down to pick a man out of the sea. Three times I watched him go down; three times he brought men up through the blackness.

I saw another helicopter almost touch the water—its rotor blades seemed to be spinning through the flames—to pick up a man in a bright orange survival suit. Lifeboats were launched from *Sir Tristram* and began taking some of the rubber life rafts in tow.

Other life rafts were drifting, taken by the wind sometimes away from the inferno, but then suddenly towards it. Pilots in the helicopters waiting at the bow saw what was happening, and immediately four of them took their machines to the rear of the ship by the flames. They came down low and, using the downdraught of their rotor blades, slowly began to push the rubber dinghies away. Slowly, yard by yard, each helicopter taking care of one dinghy full of men, they pushed them to the safety of the beach.

There was much heroism at Fitzroy, but this single tribute must be paid to the helicopter pilots and their winchmen who saved so many.'

The casualties at Bluff Cove were less than had been feared, (50 men killed), but what was more serious was the dislocation of the Welsh Guards, who were badly shaken by their ordeal and unfit to play much part in the advance on Port Stanley.

Port Stanley falls

What makes Bluff Cove so much more tragic is that it was not vital to the success of the overall plans drawn up by General Moore. The commanding heights above Port Stanley were no longer in Argentine hands, and on the night of June 14 the Argentine commander, General Mario Menendez, bowed to the inevitable and asked for a ceasefire. The following day a full surrender was signed, and to their amazement the British found that they had been facing 11 000 soldiers, rather than the 9000 originally estimated.

At first the figure of 15 000 men was reported, but this now appears to have been an error by the Argentines, possibly in translation. But whatever the exact number it was a convincing victory, in which the Argentines had been not only out-manoeuvred but completely out-fought. It went against all the precepts of amphibious warfare, in which the attackers are supposed to outnumber the defenders three-to-one if success is to be guaranteed.

The last naval casualty was the destroyer *Glamorgan*. During one of the final bombardments of Port Stanley on Friday June 11 she was lying about 19 miles offshore, moving in to fire her twin 4.5-in guns when her navigating officer, Lt-Cdr Inskip saw on the radar plot a small 'blip' travelling at high speed towards the ship. Interpreting this correctly as an Exocet, he ordered the ship to turn away from it, to reduce the target-echo. Thanks to his quick thinking there was a gap of 40 seconds during which the 6000-ton ship could swing around and present her stern to the missile.

The hulk of *Sir Galahad* continues to blaze hours after the attack. Eventually she was towed out to sea and sunk as a war grave. At first it was attempted to sink her with a Tigerfish torpedo, but this failed to explode, so the old Mk 8 non-guided torpedo was used.

After an agonizing wait there was a loud bang aft and clouds of smoke, but the ship's luck held. The Exocet had grazed the upper deck, bounced off and slewed into the helicopter hangar. The missile seems to have been right at the end of its run, and almost 'failed to make it'. There was a small detonation, enough to wreck the hangar and send a shower of deadly splinters into the galley. The occupants of the galley were killed and the Wessex helicopter in the hangar was destroyed. In all 13 men were killed and 14 were injured, and the fire which broke out took three-and-a-half hours to put out.

On July 10 the battered *Glamorgan* returned to Portsmouth. Her wrecked hangar was protected from the elements by a large tarpaulin, but apart from that her after superstructure seemed intact, further evidence to suggest that the Exocet's fuze had not functioned to full effect. She was not hit by an air-launched missile, and the Argentines had rigged up an ingenious coast-defence version of the standard MM-38 ship-launched Exocet, using the ship-launched twin-mount on a trailer.

With the fall of Port Stanley the major strain on the Task Force was lifted, but there was no chance for it to withdraw immediately. For one thing Port Stanley airfield was still out of action, so that the two carriers still carried the burden of providing air cover until such time as the runway could be lengthened to take Phantoms. For another, the Falklands were never capable of feeding 16 000 extra soldiers. It was essential to remove as many Argentine prisoners as possible, for the simple reason that housing and accommodating them was an intolerable burden. For the same reason the *QE2* and *Canberra* took as many British troops home as could be spared. It was possible to release the damaged ships, however, and a trickle of warships started the long haul back to their home ports. The first home was the destroyer *Glasgow*, proudly displaying two bomb holes in her hull, and shortly afterwards the frigate *Argonaut* arrived, with similar tales of miraculous escapes. It had been a hard war for them and their sailors, and before long other ships and crews would have their own stories to tell.

The importance of British air support

It is impossible to record in full the experiences of the Harrier and Sea Harrier and their pilots in combat over the Falklands, but it is opportune to recount the story of Flt Lt Jeffrey Glover, whose RAF Harrier GR.3 was shot down on May 21, and who became

the Argentine's only prisoner-of-war not repatriated immediately. On his return to the UK on July 10, he told reporters of his first and last operational mission from HMS *Hermes*.

The battle-scarred frigate *Argonaut* on her return on June 26. She was hit twice, once in the Seacat magazine and once in the boiler room.

'I was given the target to attack in Port Howard. I was flying over the sea and about to coast in when I was hit by three bangs in close succession. The aircraft rolled hard to starboard and I tried to correct the roll but the stick was locked. Then I was inverted and all I could see was water. I began to try to right the aircraft and the next thing I knew was the bang of the canopy going off and then I was unconscious. I woke up about four feet under water and I was swallowing mouthfuls like crazy. I couldn't see out of my right eye and I seemed to have lost my helmet. I was in shock and I remember looking for my dinghy. After a while, I realized it was still attached to my backside. Then I heard voices and saw the rowing boats. Unfortunately they were Argentinians.'

He went on to say that later 'I was introduced to the man who shot me down and I was told he did it with a Blowpipe'—a man-portable anti-aircraft missile built in Britain which was in service on both sides during the conflict.

Towards the end of the conflict, the Harriers and Sea Harriers carried out their most unusual raids of the campaign—dropping leaflets over Port Stanley urging the Argentine troops to surrender and offering a safe conduct. It was a task that the original designers of the aircraft never allowed for in all their proposals for the aircraft.

One interesting set of statistics has come out. During the conflict, the carriers were operating with a 200 per cent increase of aircraft, and only a 20 per cent increase in maintenance personnel per aircraft. The aircraft flew over 2000 sorties, which averages out at six sorties per aircraft per day, and during that time an 80 per cent availability-rate was achieved. The remarkable performance of the Sea Harriers and their RAF counterparts has still to be fully assessed, but it has at least spurred on one potential NATO customer into pushing for the aircraft. No doubt others will follow. The UK Secretary of State for Defence, John Nott, had this to say: 'The performance of the Sea and RAF Harriers in this contest has been remarkable. The skill of our pilots has been immense and the Harrier has proved itself to have been an exceptional aircraft.'

There can also be no doubt that without the helicopter, the campaign in the Falklands would have taken longer and cost more in men's lives and materiél. From the first reconnaissance sorties of the *Endurance* flight's Wasps, the landings on South Georgia, the attack on the *Somellera*, the landings at Port San Carlos, the rescue missions at Bluff Cove and the sheer grind of supporting troop movements, re-supply, reconnaissance, casevac (service jargon for casualty evacuation), maintaining an ASW screen around the Fleet and acting as decoys for Exocet missiles, the helicopters were everywhere. It will be some time before one can chronicle the full story of their role, for it is only the more spectacular incidents and missions which have been given the publicity to date.

In anti-submarine warfare (ASW), the lack of reported activity is perhaps the best indicator of its effectiveness. Apart from the destruction of the *Santa Fé*, there were no banner headlines about Argentine submarines being sunk, or attacking the Task Force, or what was more worrying to Admiral Woodward, the QE2, on her way into and out of the War Zone.

The Sea King was the principal ASW helicopter of the Fleet Air Arm, being a hunter and killer of submarines. For the former role she was equipped with a dipping sonar and a number of

The assault ships *Fearless* and *Intrepid* are basically mobile floating docks which trim down by flooding their ballast tanks. The photograph on the left shows how Landing Craft Mechanized (LCMs) dock and undock inside their 11 000-ton hulls. *Above,* an empty LCM approaches the stern well of the *Fearless* during the landings on San Carlos. On the far left is Michael Nicholson, ITN's reporter, in the thick of the fight.

A Mirage IIIE *(right)* comes in low over the San Carlos anchorage. These supersonic strike aircraft were handled superbly in a series of near-suicidal attacks on British ships. On D-Day (May 21), the Argentine Air Force put 72 aircraft over the invasion beachhead. *Above,* a bomb nearly hits the RFA *Resource.* Despite heavy Argentine losses, a large number of ships were hit and *Ardent, Antelope* and *Coventry* eventually sank. A Sea King *(far right)* passes over the wreck of HMS *Antelope* on May 23. The bomb which exploded in her engine room the night before probably detonated her Seacat missile magazine and torpedo store, destroying her superstructure, and breaking the ship's back. She sank in a cloud of smoke and steam

The deceptive calm of the San Carlos landings (*above* and *right*) in between air attacks. An Army Gazelle helicopter with supplies slung underneath passes a frigate, and camouflaged landing craft approach a landing ship. In the background (*right*) a Sea King is well camouflaged against the shore, the steepness of which shows how difficult it was for Argentine pilots to sweep in low to attack. Disaster, however, struck at Bluff Cove (*far right*).

The bombs which hit *Sir Galahad* in the engine room set her on fire, and helicopters moved in dramatically and immediately to rescue soldiers and civilian crewmen. Lieutenant John Miller was commended for outstanding bravery in rescuing this man *(left)* hanging below the Sea King in his survival suit. Wessex helicopters used the downdraught of their rotors *(far left)* to drive inflatable rafts towards the shore.

Argentine losses throughout the campaign were heavy, especially in aircraft. *Above* is a wrecked Pucara. This twin-engined counter-insurgency aircraft was very effective against British land forces, and destroying them was given priority. When the Argentine land forces retreated they left much materiél behind, like this twin 35 mm mobile anti-aircraft gun *(right)*.

sonobuoys, while for the latter role, the new Marconi Stingray lightweight torpedo was rushed to the Task Force, and four of these (or the earlier Mk 46 torpedo) could be carried. To detect submarines, the dipping sonar is lowered from the helicopter, which is hovering some 50-100 ft above the surface of the sea, and a sonar search is made. If a contact is made, then a torpedo is dropped, to home in on the contact.

At least four Sea Kings carried an additional ASW aid in the form of an airborne ASW magnetometer or Magnetic Anomoly Detector (MAD). This is a specially equipped drogue towed behind the helicopter, with equipment installed to detect a change in the magnetic field of the area; such a change indicating the possible presence of a submarine.

The Sea Kings were used as part of the Task Force ASW screen, integrating with the shipborne sonars and filling gaps where necessary. ASW work is demanding on the aircrew at the best of times, and to conduct such operations in the terrible conditions of a South Atlantic winter is a tribute to all ASW crews.

The other airborne arm of the ASW screen were the Lynx and Wasp helicopters operating from frigates and destroyers. These helicopters could carry two torpedoes of the types already mentioned, and were directed on to contacts by their mother ship or either a Sea King or RAF Nimrod. There are no official reports of these helicopters being in action in this role, although, as is the case with the Sea King, there is no doubt that they were in full use through the conflict.

While the main landings were seaborne, the Sea King HC.4 and Wessex HU.5 helicopters played a major part in ferrying troops ashore as well as equipment. During the crossing of the island of East Falkland, the troops went on foot ('Yomping' as the Marines called it) to leave the helicopters free to support them with supplies, ammunition and equipment. Once in control of the high ground around Port Stanley, it was helicopters which brought up the 105-mm Light Guns for the artillery bombardment of the town, and kept them re-supplied with ammunition.

The helicopters were also involved in the landing and removal of special forces around the islands, and if one reads between the lines of the loss of the Sea King over Chile, into Tierra del Fuego on the mainland. They certainly landed the assault group which attacked Pebble Island in a classic commando-style raid on the night of May 14.

Despite persistent rumours that seven SAS men were being held prisoner in Argentina this was never confirmed. There was also fantastic speculation that 12 men had been landed by Sea King to operate remote-controlled monitoring equipment which signalled the whereabouts of Argentine aircraft to the Task Force via an American satellite.

If there is a kernel of truth in these rumours it may be that air strikes from Rio Gallegos were reported. It is also possible that some attempt was made to sabotage the small number of Super Etendards.

Army Air Corps Scout helicopters were used to deploy teams of Gurkhas around the islands to mop up and take the surrender of isolated pockets of Argentine troops, while the single RAF Chinook to survive the *Atlantic Conveyor*'s loss was worked to full stretch.

The Army Air Corps were also involved on reconnaissance duties for the ground forces, and two Gazelles were lost to Argentine Blowpipe SAMs during the push out of the San Carlos bridgehead. A Scout was also shot down during the attack on Goose Green and Darwin. Again, their role was mostly unsung, but necessary and certainly used to full effect.

The Argentine Navy
When the whole campaign was over one question remained unanswered. What had happened to the Argentine Navy? In particular, why had their submarines played so little part in the war at sea? The questions are all the more perplexing when it is borne in mind that the Commander-in-Chief of the Navy, Admiral Jorge Anaya, is believed to have been one of the prime movers in the original invasion. His ships had been sent to sea to support the 'scrap-merchants', and they had been taken to South Georgia in the Navy transport *Bahia Buen Suceso*.

With so many contradictory rumours coming out of Argentina it is still not possible to say whether the Navy felt unable to put to sea because of the British blockade or because Admiral Anaya wished to maintain a 'fleet in being'. The pressure on the Navy to make some sort of gesture, however futile, must have been great, particularly when the Air Force losses became so heavy at the end of May. The British were convinced that the Argentine Navy would put to sea before the end, bent on a 'death-ride' to achieve some sort of spectacular success against the Task Force.

The sole survivor of the *Atlantic Conveyor*'s Chinook HC.1 helicopters—'Bravo November'—prepares to lift an underslung ammunition load while two armourers tow two 1000-lb 'iron' bombs on the flight deck.

Another theory is that the Navy was kept intact to provide a power-base for the admirals for the political struggle which would inevitably follow the defeat of the Army in the Falklands, or even for a war against Chile.

There is, however, a rational explanation for the failure of the aircraft carrier *Vienticinco de Mayo* to get to sea, even if there had been no British blockade. She was about to receive Super Etendard strike aircraft, as we know, but this would require a new steam catapult and other modifications to her flight deck. The catapult had not been delivered (it is still in the UK), but work is likely to have started on the overhaul, and this would have made the ship unfit to operate an air group, even if she could put to sea.

The following Argentine merchant vessels *are* known to have operated in the Falklands and in the vicinity of the Task Force:

Bahia Buen Suceso
3828-ton naval transport, used to land the scrap dealers on South Georgia, and subsequently landed troops. Damaged twice, once by Sea Harriers in Fox Bay and on May 17 by gunfire.

Bahia Pariso
An unidentified ship, probably requisitioned for conversion to a covert intelligence-gatherer (AGI). She shadowed HMS *Endurance* in the days before the Argentine invasion, and British sources suspect that she is another ship operating under a new name.

Rio de la Plata
10 409 GRT requisitioned merchantman, used as an AGI to shadow the *Canberra* south of Ascension. She was chased from the scene by HMS *Antelope*.

Narwal
2480 GRT Polish-built factory trawler, requisitioned for use as an AGI inside the TEZ. Badly damaged by Sea Harriers and captured by RN boarding parties. Later sank in tow to South Georgia, May 10.

Isla de Estados
Chartered transport sunk May 12 by HMS *Alacrity*.

Rio Carcaran
8000 GRT chartered transport set on fire by bombs and gunfire in Port King Bay.

Monsunen
Falklands Trading Co coaster forced ashore May 23.

There were four Argentine submarines in nominal commission at the outset of the campaign, two elderly ex-American 'Guppy' boats, the *Santa Fe* and *Santiago del Estero*, and two modern German-built Type 209 boats, the *Salta* and *San Luis*. The *Santa Fe*, as we know, was severely disabled at South Georgia but to get her to sea the sister had been 'cannibalized'. However, to maintain an illusion that she was still seaworthy the hull was towed from port to port.

In theory the Type 209 boats should have posed a major threat to the Task Force. With the British nuclear boats limited to the 12-mile Total Exclusion Zone (by reason of their deep draught, as well as by order) there should on paper be no reason why these small, manoeuvrable and silent-running craft should not have been able to get to sea unobserved. From that a logical deduction is that they would not or could not. According to reliable American sources the 209s could not put to sea because of an appallingly high number of mechanical problems. They were simply unprepared for war.

The only major submarine alarm reported by the Task Force was the one on May 4, after the sinking of HMS *Sheffield*, and the counter-attacks by *Invincible*'s ASW screen may, of course, have sunk the submarine. There is also a persistent rumour in British circles that a submarine was sunk in Falkland Sound by an Ikara anti-submarine missile.

The weakness of this story is that British official sources have made no mention of any such sinking, not even after hostilities had ended. This could, of course, be a form of psychological warfare, refusing to confirm the loss in order to raise doubts about the reliability of the remaining submarine, but it is a refinement altogether too fanciful to be true.

Another version of the rumour has the submarine hiding on the bottom of Falkland Sound in the hope of ambushing the British ships, but remaining there because of a mechanical fault until finally her crew became asphyxiated. There are also reports of a clandestine operation against one of the submarines by SAS or SBS detachments, but like all such reports there can be no way of confirming them.

What is certain is that the performance of the *Armada Republica Argentina* is in total contrast to the reckless heroism of the Air Force and the dogged determination shown by many of the soldiers in the Falklands. The Army may not have been well led but the victorious British were generous in their praise for its willingness to fight hard.

Chapter 6

Lessons for the Future

The lessons of the Falklands War are legion despite a British victory; some of them cannot be talked about, if only for the reason that we do not know how some specific items of equipment functioned. Nor are we privileged to know what the two governments and their military advisers actually intended. Having said that it is still possible to look at the more obvious points which have emerged.

The role of the Navy

The most important point concerns the role of the Royal Navy. As we pointed out at the beginning of this book, the Royal Navy has shrunk in size over the past 30 years, and formally renounced its 'East of Suez' role at the end of the 1960s. It has devoted itself to the principal task of anti-submarine warfare in the Eastern Atlantic, and recent warships built have an exclusively anti-submarine role.

It was fortuitous that a number of ships of the 'Old Navy' were still left, for these proved the most useful units of the Task Force. Under this heading can be included the carrier *Hermes*, the assault ships, *Fearless* and *Intrepid* and many of the older DLGs and frigates, all of which were under sentence of death from the present Secretary of State for Defence.

What had gone for good was the might of traditional carrier air power, as represented by the *Ark Royal* until 1978. Although much had been made of the flexibility of the Sea Harriers, they lacked the performance and punch of the *Ark*'s Phantom interceptors and Buccaneer bombers. And without the *Ark*'s Gannet airborne early warning aircraft the Sea Harriers were at a great disadvantage.

The Task Force, then, was not an ideal 'mix' of ships for its job, and its performance must be judged in that light. What tipped the scale in Britain's favour was the high degree of training, and the happy coincidence that the normal theatre of operations, the North Atlantic, had at least demanded seaworthy ships. It was also of tremendous benefit that the land forces had trained in very similar terrain.

Airborne early warning

The lack of airborne early warning radar showed itself during the bitter air battles over the San Carlos beachhead. Time and again the Argentine attackers came in low over the hills, and as they were never detected until the last minute there was a constant risk that the Sea Harriers would be caught in the wrong position.

Two other events demonstrated just as forcibly how important AEW is to a modern fleet. The first was the sinking of the *Sheffield*; a timely warning of the approach of the Super Etendards could have enabled the Sea Harriers to at least distract them from their attack, possibly forcing them to break off before firing. Better still, they could have destroyed the reconnaissance aircraft which was tracking the Task Force, and if that had been done in time the Super Etendards would have lacked the data essential for firing their rockets. The other example is less obvious; the Argentine Air Force could have been prevented from detecting the Task Force after Ascension if the reconnaissance plan had been detected at maximum range, denying them vital intelligence for a few more days.

Clearly the clock cannot be put back; the Royal Navy cannot renege on its commitment to NATO and go back to being an international police force. Even if the political will were there the cost would be hard to justify as there are (fortunately) very few British overseas possessions which need that sort of protection. The Royal Navy has an overriding requirement to contribute to the defence of the United Kingdom, and until such time as membership of NATO fails to secure that defence, NATO must have the first call on Britain's naval forces.

On the other hand, there is a growing concern inside NATO and elsewhere that the current provisions of the North Atlantic Treaty, limiting operations to specific geographical areas, are unrealistic. The critics argue that NATO and its European members rely on raw materials from outside the NATO area, and that some form of protection for ships carrying those raw materials should be provided. This, of course, means principally oil. The continuing Gulf War between Iraq and Iran, and the earlier crisis over the American Embassy hostages in Teheran show how quickly the West's oil-supplies can be threatened.

Another flash-point is Libya; the clash between the US Navy and the Libyan Air Force last year proves that NATO could very easily be faced with the need to convoy merchant ships through the Central Mediterranean. Just like the Falklands conflict, such an operation would carry with it the risk of attack from the most sophisticated anti-ship missiles.

The ability to operate 'out of theatre', to use the current military jargon, is therefore not incompatible with NATO's interests. Yet the excuse for denying the Royal Navy its vital AEW aircraft has been since 1966 the assertion that in the North Atlantic there would always be sufficient air cover from shore-based maritime patrol aircraft.

NATO is introducing the E-3 Sentry Airborne Warning and Control System (AWACS) aircraft and the Royal Air Force will shortly receive its first AEW Nimrod aircraft, which will make a vast improvement to early warning over North-western Europe. Naval aviators recognize the great value of shore-based aircraft and AWACS in particular to naval operations, but remind us that even in the North Atlantic the grounding of a single aircraft from engine-trouble can leave a huge gap in the 'umbrella', through which hostile aircraft and ships can slip. A shipborne AEW system would enable naval forces to cope with such an eventuality at immediate notice.

The failure to provide the Royal Navy with an AEW aircraft is thus linked to the broader question of whether NATO's requirements are being met in the most suitable form. There is also the question of how to provide such an aircraft. The Royal Navy, since the demise of its big carriers, has enthusiastically embraced the Sea Harrier jump-jet, and has built ships to operate it. But the main problem of STOVL aircraft is lack of range, and to remedy this the 'ski-jump' has been adopted.

This simple device increases payload (whether in the form of weapons or fuel) but it also means that the flight deck is no longer useable by conventional aircraft for takeoff. As a result, although it might have been possible to refurbish the old Gannet AEW

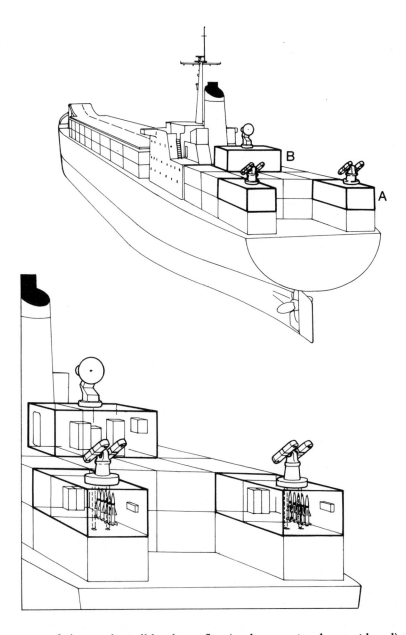

To increase the number of aircraft/helicopter operating platforms available to the Task Force, the merchant vessels *Atlantic Conveyor* and *Atlantic Causeway* were equipped with flight decks and were most effective. These drawings show an advanced proposal for the installation of a flight deck with 'ski-jump' ramp and a containerized BAeD Lightweight Seawolf point-defence missile system. Twin mountings (A) can be seen on either aft quarter with the VM40 (B) tracker system (now dropped in favour of a Marconi solution) mounted centrally behind the funnel.

aircraft during the Falklands conflict (and was seriously considered) they could not fly off her deck. Another emergency measure considered was to recommission the old commando carrier *Bulwark* to act simply as a 'spare deck'. The 30-year-old 'Rusty B' had retained her flat deck, but like *Hermes* had lost her arrester wires; had those been available she might have been put to use, and with three or four Gannets also reprieved from the scrapheap might have served her turn.

A more practical short-term solution is to fit a surveillance radar in a Sea King helicopter, and this is being pursued actively by the Fleet Air Arm in conjunction with Westland Helicopters. In answer to the question of why it was not done before, it can only be said that political approval had not been forthcoming. A helicopter is not ideal for such a mission because it lacks endurance and altitude, but in the Falklands anything would have been better than no cover at all.

This solution has now been adopted by the Royal Navy. In 11 weeks, Westland Helicopters, Thorn–EMI and the MoD worked together to produce what must be an interim AEW helicopter. Based on the Sea King HAS.2 airframe, a Searchwater radar (as used on the Nimrod MR.2 retrofit programme) has been pod-mounted on the starboard side of the Sea King. This swivels aft for takeoff and landing. Two out of the five reported conversions are now aboard HMS *Illustrious*, which has replaced *Invincible* in the South Atlantic.

Yet another solution would have been to equip the air-defence ships with a three-dimensional radar. A '3-D' radar provides simultaneous range, bearing and height of incoming targets, and although the height data obtained is never very accurate it is good enough to allow a Sea Harrier to be vectored to a point where its own radar can take over.

American observers have always wondered at the Royal Navy's prejudice against 3-D radars, which are fitted to all US Navy destroyers. It is known that at least one British radar company offered a 3-D radar to the Royal Navy ten years ago, but it was turned down as 'not required'.

The real long-term answer is to design a STOVL airframe capable of lifting a suitable radar and keeping it aloft for a reasonable time. The first major development from the Harrier is the US Marine Corps' AV-8B Harrier II, and it is being bought for the RAF to replace its GR.3 Harriers. Studies could be initiated by McDonnell Douglas, the makers, to see if an AEW variant is feasible, but the provision of a very small number of aircraft, possibly only six, would make it a costly business. Grumman Aerospace is working on a tilt-wing aircraft which might also be suitable in the AEW role and Bell's XV-15 tilt rotor craft is also being developed to include, among others, AEW. However, these aircraft have not yet flown, so it would be an even longer-term solution than the AV-8B.

The problem of fires

The loss of HMS *Sheffield* followed by the losses in Falkland Sound of the frigates *Ardent* and *Antelope* and the destroyer *Coventry* raised an immediate outcry because of the speed with which they caught fire. It was argued that the *Sheffield* might well have survived if the fire had not taken hold so fiercely. If anything evidence points the other way. Two ships, the frigate *Plymouth* and the DLG *Glamorgan*, both caught fire (in *Glamorgan*'s case, two fires started). In both ships the fires were put out very quickly, and there seems little reason to suspect furnishings as the main cause of the fires in *Sheffield*, *Ardent*, *Antelope* and *Coventry*.

The problem of fire-protection does need urgent attention, however. There is no doubt that too much inflammable material has crept into warships in an effort to mitigate the inherent discomfort. On the other hand it is too much to ask people to live in an environment devoid of creature comforts. To quote a veteran of the Second World War, 'one might as well be sunk in comfort'.

A balance must be found but it is too early to say exactly what solution will be chosen; even so smoke-generating materials such as foam-rubber and PVC *must* be eliminated. There are many flameproof materials such as carbonized or oxidized fibre on the market, and these must be introduced as soon as possible. Rechargeable CO_2 extinguishers have been rushed to the Task Force, and 15 000 sets of Emergency Life Support Apparatus (ELSA) smoke-proof breathing sets have been ordered.

Much was made of the use of aluminium in the ships which sank, but the criticism was mostly ill-informed. There are, as we have seen, technical objections to the use of aluminium in warships, but they are matters of emphasis rather than any reflection on the competence of the design itself. Nor is the use of aluminium and light alloys an unorthodox or risky novelty. Large liners such as the *Canberra* and the *QE2* are able to have an extra deck of passenger-accommodation because of light alloy. However, while using steel instead of aluminium in a ship's superstructure will not stop a missile (as the sinking of the *Sheffield* and *Coventry* showed), it may localize a fire once the ship is hit. Aluminium can actually make a fire worse *after* the ship has been hit.

There are two classic examples of what can go wrong with aluminium structures, both of which happened since the Type 21 frigates were built. The first was the case of the cruiser USS *Worden*, which was cruising off Vietnam when a Phantom aircraft inadvertently released a Shrike anti-radiation missile. The missile armed itself and performed exactly as designed, homing on the radar-pulses from the *Worden's* main search radar. It exploded about 80 ft overhead, showering the cruiser's superstructure with fragments; the ship was plunged into darkness as the lethal fragments sheared through electrical cables and radar waveguides. For six hours the cruiser was out of action while casualties were tended and damage-control parties repaired the damage.

The 'softness' of the aluminium superstructure had been foreseen, and nobody was surprised that the waveguides had been so efficiently severed by the Shrike's comparatively small warhead, for that was what it was intended to do. What caused much more alarm was the realization that some 60 per cent of the damage had been done by fragments of aluminium—it was estimated later that for every fragment of warhead the aluminium panels had generated two more. In other words, the superstructure, instead of shielding the ship, was assisting in her destruction.

Two years later, a similar missile cruiser, the USS *Belknap* suffered a more spectacular disaster off the coast of Sicily when she collided with the carrier *John F Kennedy* during an exercise. The *Belknap* was caught by the overhang of the carrier's flight deck, and a fuel jettison pipe which fractured, poured an estimated 1000 gallons of jet fuel over her superstructure. All that was needed was a spark from metal grinding against metal, and the cruiser was quickly engulfed in flames.

When the fires were finally extinguished the *Belknap* had burned down to the weather deck, and virtually all of her lofty bridgework and plated masts had disappeared. In fact the disaster, although spectacular, had less bearing on ship-design than the accident to the *Worden*, for no warship would be fit to fight after being sluiced with a thousand gallons of blazing liquid.

In 1977 the British frigate *Amazon*, lead-ship of the Type 21 ships, had a narrow escape when an electrical fire started under the floor of her Operations Room. Fire-parties found that aluminium ladderways had melted in the heat, making it impossible to get to the heart of the blaze. The ship was lucky to avoid the fate of the *Belknap* because the sprinkler-system put the fire out, but it brought home to the Royal Navy the risks of using too much aluminium.

It has been suggested during the Falklands campaign that aluminium was introduced because the introduction of gas-turbine propulsion since 1967 had made warships top-heavy, but this is simply untrue. The *Sheffield* class (Type 42), the *Amazon* class (Type 21) and the *Broadsword* class (Type 22) all have Rolls-Royce gas turbines, but only the *Amazon* class have aluminium super-structures.

Modern warship defence

The defence of modern warships lies in preventing the missile from hitting, and to that end she is equipped with 'passive' defences loosely described under the heading of Electronic Warfare. These take the form of decoys, Electronic Support Measures (ESM) and Electronic Counter Measures (ECM).

The standard chaff system in the Royal Navy is the Corvus Mk 3 rocket-launcher, which fires a spread of eight rockets to generate a cloud of metallic particles, similar in principle to the 'Window' first used by the RAF in the Second World War. ESM analyzes radio- and radar-pulses to give the receiving ship some warning of the nature of the threat. For example it can tell the listener that he is under surveillance from an X-Band radar, and provided that the electronic 'memory' can identify it, the type and even the nationality of the transmitting radar can be known. Every radar has its own 'signature', and provided that this signature is known, its characteristics can be stored in the ESM equipment's memory.

The ESM is divided into active and passive equipment, or in simple language, jammers or equipment for modifying the radar image 'seen' by the enemy radar. It is therefore nonsense to talk of the 'unstoppable Exocet missile', and the question must be asked, could HMS *Sheffield* have avoided being sunk? The answer must be yes, provided that certain requirements were met.

First, it must be asked if the Naval Intelligence Department had provided the Task Force with adequate warning that the Argentines had the air-launched AM-39 Exocet? The sale of the AM-39 to Argentina had not been announced by the manufacturers, but as they were known to be buying the Super Etendard (for which the AM-39 was designed) it should have been a logical deduction. Prior to the Argentine invasion in April there appears to have been very little attempt to monitor military developments in Argentina, and this would explain the lapse. The British seem to have believed that as long as no Aérospatiale experts were in Argentina nothing could happen, but worse and more astounding, they had no idea of the maximum range of a Super Etendard.

There is evidence to suggest that the Royal Navy has been

HMS Sheffield Type 42 Destroyer

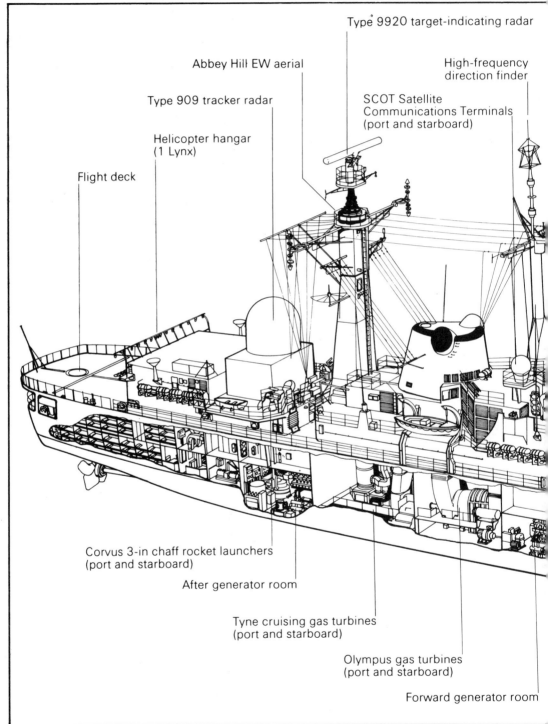

Type 9920 target-indicating radar

Abbey Hill EW aerial

High-frequency direction finder

Type 909 tracker radar

SCOT Satellite Communications Terminals (port and starboard)

Helicopter hangar (1 Lynx)

Flight deck

Corvus 3-in chaff rocket launchers (port and starboard)

After generator room

Tyne cruising gas turbines (port and starboard)

Olympus gas turbines (port and starboard)

Forward generator room

interrogator

Type 965/966 'Double Bedstead'
air-warning radar

20-mm Mk 7 Oerlikon gun
(port and starboard wheelhouse)

Type 909 tracker radar
(inside weatherproof dome)

Operations room
(below wheelhouse)

Sea Dart Mod 1 twin arm launcher

4.5-in Mk 8 gun

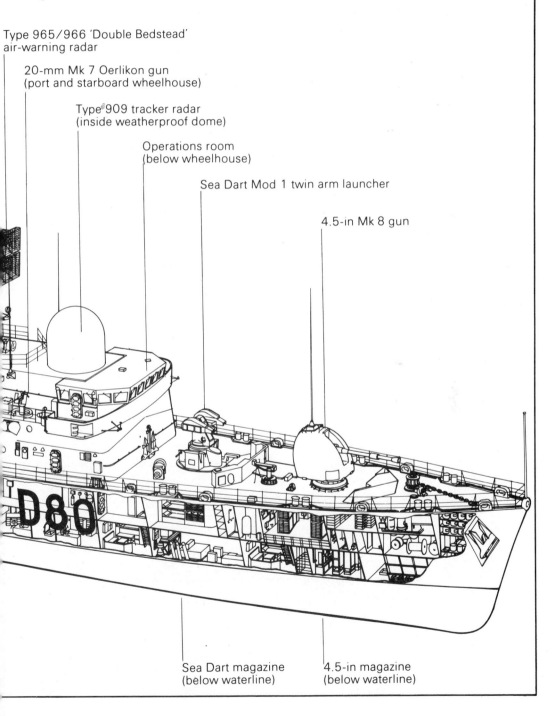

D80

Sea Dart magazine
(below waterline)

4.5-in magazine
(below waterline)

Lack of space in the Type 42 design resulted in a very crowded Operations Room. This view of *Coventry*'s Ops Room shows the vertical and horizontal displays on which the data from various of the ship's radars are shown.

slow to modernize its electronic warfare equipment. Foreign observers are by and large unimpressed by the sort of equipment still used, and even that has been very slow in reaching the Fleet. HMS *Sheffield*, for example, spent the first six years without the standard Abbey Hill electronic warfare equipment, and the first photograph showing it installed was taken in February 1981. Other ships like HMS *Arrow* went to the Falklands without it. Abbey Hill is in any case only an amalgamation of two earlier pieces of commercial ECM and ESM equipment, and the vital IFF (Identification Friend or Foe) element has never been added.

The main weakness of the Type 42 destroyers in electronic warfare was a result of their cramped dimensions, for the Operations Room turned out to be too small to allow the ESM and ECM to be integrated with the main Action Information Organization (AIO). Thus when the ship's ESM detected the approach of the Exocet there was a fatal time-lag before the information could be interpreted and acted upon.

How such a sophisticated ship came to be built with insufficient space for an efficient Ops Room has already been described in Chapter 3, but lack of internal space does not explain away inadequacies of some British equipment.

For years the British Ministry of Defence's Procurement Executive has been a byword for inefficiency, mainly through the inordinate time taken to get equipment into service. In the words of Kenneth Warren MP, 'it is a magnificent organization for spending money on Defence, but it is not very good at procuring equipment for the Armed Forces.' The equipment is often obsolescent by the time it gets into service, no matter how good it was when first designed fifteen years earlier.

The big 'double bedstead' Type 965 air-warning radar fitted in the *Sheffield* class destroyers is a good example of this. It was designed in the early 1950s, and has a very slow data-rate, giving it poor performance against high-speed targets. Operating on a long waveband (P-Band, or 1.4 metres, to be precise), it has reasonable range and definition of high-flying targets but was never intended to cope with modern targets. Its replacement, called Type 1030, was very slow in development (it was finally cancelled in 1981) and in desperation the Marconi antenna was fitted to Dutch processing equipment, to form the interim Type 1022. Even this 'lash-up' was so slow in development that it was only available for the last four of the Type 42 destroyers.

Working with Type 965 is the target-indicating Type 992Q S-Band (centimetric) radar, which designates targets for guns and missiles. For years it has been known that without a feature called Moving Target Indication (MTI) this radar would not be good at tracking targets against 'clutter', the interference caused by nearby land ('land-clutter') or rain- and snow-showers ('sea-clutter'). British radar manufacturers offered to retrofit MTI to these radars but nothing was done. All that was done was a very modest update of the processing equipment of the Type 965 radar, after which it was renumbered Type 966 to suggest some sort of major improvement.

The outcome of this parsimony has been that the Task Force ships were repeatedly taken by surprise, as their radars were unable to track the Argentine Mirages and Skyhawks with any precision. The heavy losses sustained during the San Carlos landings must at least partly be blamed on the late response by the ship's defences. Coupled with the lack of airborne early warning radar it was nearly fatal.

Naval missile systems

We have already seen that ships were built too small to accommodate adequate defence systems but there are disturbing questions to be answered about some of the systems themselves. The elderly Seacat close-range system was found to be outclassed, whereas its successor Seawolf worked very well.

Sea Dart, on the other hand, proved very slow to respond. Once again, parsimony combined with an unrealistic appreciation of the conditions under which the missile would function led to unpardonable restrictions. The launcher designed for the Type 42 destroyers was given a hand-operated chain hoist—precisely why, we do not know, but almost certainly the reasons were associated with cost or weight. The engineers working on the missile questioned the absence of any power-operated hoist, but were told by the Procurement Executive committee not to worry.

There was also a delay in Sea Dart's firing circuit, to give time for the missile to warm up although this has been publicly denied by the manufacturers. All missiles need this delay; Exocet, for example, takes 60 seconds to warm up the magnetron in the homing head, and a further 36 seconds to spin and align the gyroscopes. With Sea Dart the waiting time is complicated by a Naval Explosive Regulation (NER) which prohibits any missile from being 'brought to life' in the magazine. The vital pieces of equipment in the Sea Dart which need this warm-up are two oscillators, and taken in conjunction with the laborious process of loading, the Sea Dart system as it stands is not ideal for coping with attacks in quick succession.

A major problem encountered in the South Atlantic was with optically tracked weapons, specifically Rapier and Seawolf. In the intense cold the exhaust gas of the rocket motor condensed in a white cloud. Normally the weapon-aimer tracks the missile by following the red glow of its motor, but this dense cloud effectively hid the whole missile at times. The only counter was to fly the missile across the field of view, a process which took longer and involved some loss of accuracy.

There were other problems with missiles, and one eyewitness talked of them 'switching themselves off' and 'tumbling drunkenly out of their launchers' into the sea. Paradoxically there may have been too much *and* too little faith in electronics. On the one hand, missiles were expected to do everything at the press of a button, but equally there was a reluctance to use some of the systems to full advantage.

It is obvious that Britain was fortunate not to lose more men and equipment. Indeed afterwards the Chief of Defence Staff, Admiral Sir Terence Lewin, admitted that allowance had been made for heavier losses, even one of the carriers. Amidst this chronicle of failures and lucky escapes, it must not be forgotten that many systems worked very well indeed. The Sea Harriers were not only flown outstandingly well; their Blue Fox radar performed far better than the Fleet Air Arm had hoped. The load on the pilots and the maintainers was almost beyond belief, and there were surprisingly few accidental losses. This is particularly so of the helicopters; a Sea King is normally required to have 14 hours of maintenance for every hour of flying. Towards the end of the campaign HMS *Hermes* reported that one of her Sea Harriers had flown the 1000th sortie off her deck, and in all both carriers flew off over 2000 sorties.

Successes of the campaign

One aspect which had caused a lot of worry at the start of the campaign was the strain on machinery, for the warships could only receive minor repairs at Ascension. Although clearly the state of elderly steam machinery in ships like the *Hermes*, *Fearless*, and *Intrepid* must have given their engineers grey hairs at times, there were no reports of major breakdowns. One of the hidden blessings is the amount of standardization in naval machinery; the *Leander* class frigates have a well tried steam plant which has been steadily refined since the 1950s, while the Type 21, Type 22 and Type 42 ships all use the Rolls-Royce Olympus and Tyne gas turbines. Even the *Invincible* uses the same basic type of Olympus turbine as the frigates, making the provision of machinery spares much simpler than ever before.

The despised gun proved much more important than anyone had predicted. The 4.5-in guns are reported to have fired over 8000 rounds, giving some idea of the intensity of the bombardments. Clearly the design of the Vickers 4.5-in Mk 8, with its cool propellant and emphasis on reliability stood up to prolonged firing, although several ships' guns now need relining. Those ships which retained the 40-mm Bofors gun were luckier than some, but even the 20-mm Oerlikon proved useful in repelling air attacks (it had been declared obsolete in 1945). Destroyers going out to the Falklands were hurriedly fitted with extra 20-mm gun platforms, and two Phalanx 20-mm 'Gatling' guns were mounted on the flight deck of HMS *Illustrious*, second of the *Invincible* class.

On a lighter note many observers regretted that the venerable Seaslug anti-aircraft missile had not ended its distinguished career by shooting down a live target. The DLG *Glamorgan* tried to remedy this by firing one of her Seaslug Mk 2 missiles (weighing a ton without boosters) at the Port Stanley defences.

The new carrier *Illustrious* arriving at Portsmouth on June 21. She was hurriedly armed with two 20-mm Phalanx Gatlings for close-in defence against Exocets (one can be seen alongside the Sea Dart launcher and the other right aft). Another possible solution to the sea-skimming missile is the new Contraves Seaguard system using a unique quadruple 25-mm gun mounting, a missile-detecting radar and a separate tracker.

Her sister *Antrim* put her Seaslugs to even more ingenious use. Faced with multiple targets which were clearly beyond the tracking-capability of the Type 901 radar, her ordnance artificers modified the fuzing system and used the missiles to fire a barrage, in the hope of breaking up the Argentines' formation. The sight of Seaslug's four 1/4-ton boosters blowing clear must have been disconcerting, and one Mirage was very nearly hit by a spent booster rocket.

British warships have been criticized in the past for putting too much emphasis on seakeeping, but in the appalling weather conditions of the South Atlantic nobody can have echoed that criticism. Although comfort by itself is not an important criterion for a warship, the operation of electronic systems for long periods requires a degree of steadiness. During the Second World War the provision of stabilizers was found to improve gunnery, and there can be no doubt that a steady ship functions more efficiently. There is also the question of handling helicopters, for even in good weather landing on a small flight deck is risky; in rough weather the operation can be highly dangerous.

There can be no doubt that the recapture of the Falklands was a military operation which will be quoted in textbooks for many years to come. To take a large force of warships and supply ships at short notice a distance of 8000 miles, and at the end to land in the face of heavy air attacks and defeat an enemy outnumbering the attackers by more than two-to-one is a remarkable achievement by any standards.

Ascension Island

But it must be said that without Ascension Island it is doubtful that the Task Force could have achieved its objective. It was the forward operations base for all three services, but most of all for the RAF. It was on Wideawake Airfield on Ascension that the RAF based its Victor K.2 aerial tankers and Nimrod MR.2 maritime reconnaissance and ASW aircraft. It was the turnround point for the aerial re-supply operations conducted by RAF C-130K Hercules C.1/3 and VC.10 C.1 transport aircraft. One Chinook HC.1 and a pair of Westland Sea King HAR.3 helicopters were deployed there to supplement the Navy's helicopters for vertical replenishment (vertrep) of the Fleet and SAR duties. It was also the base for the ten or so Vulcan B.2 bombers and reconnaissance aircraft and a number of Phantom FGR.2 air-defence fighters.

One of the aspects of the conflict which was (rightly) played down at the time was that of materiél assistance by the United States to the UK Government, after throwing their support behind the British action. It is well reported that further supplies of AIM-9L Sidewinder were made available. What is not so well-known is that some of these were fitted to Nimrod MR.2s for self-defence purposes, making it the largest 'fighter' in RAF service.

Other missiles supplied to the UK included the FIM-92A Stinger shoulder-launched SAM (because it was lighter to carry than the UK Blowpipe); the AGM-84A air-launched version of the Harpoon anti-ship missile (carried in the bomb-bay of the Nimrods); and the AGM-45A Shrike anti-radiation missile. The latter were acquired to deal with the land-based air defence radars on the Falklands. The Vulcans were equipped to carry two under each wing (on the old Skybolt hard points).

It is understood that at least one raid was made using these weapons. The Vulcan which landed at Rio de Janeiro (XM597 of 44 Sqn) had, in fact, been down to Port Stanley and launched two Shrikes against the Argentine TPS-43 radar there. However, because the radar was switched off after the missiles had been launched, they failed to lock on to the radiation source in time to home on to their target. The Vulcan then tried to jettison the remaining two missiles. One of these 'hung up' and, it is thought,

British Aerospace Sea Harrier FRS.1

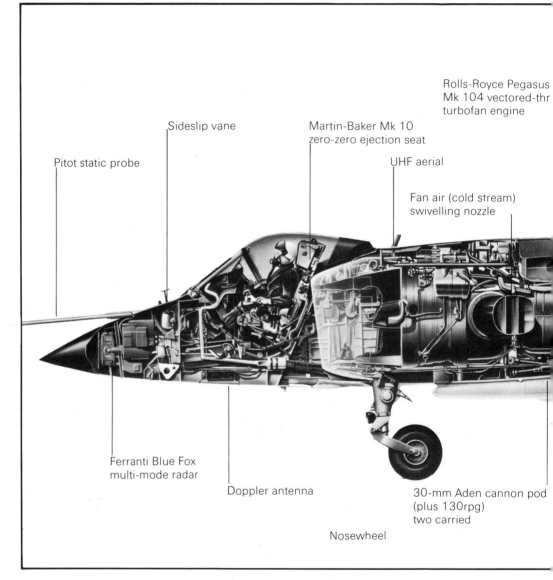

Rolls-Royce Pegasus
Mk 104 vectored-thr
turbofan engine

Sideslip vane

Martin-Baker Mk 10
zero-zero ejection seat

Pitot static probe

UHF aerial

Fan air (cold stream)
swivelling nozzle

Ferranti Blue Fox
multi-mode radar

Doppler antenna

30-mm Aden cannon pod
(plus 130rpg)
two carried

Nosewheel

because of the potential safety hazard during an air-to-air refuelling, the Victor tanker refused to 'top up' the Vulcan's tanks. The Vulcan then had no alternative but to divert to Rio where the Shrike (diplomatically referred to as a Sidewinder AAM for self defence) was impounded.

That air power played a major part in the Falklands Conflict cannot be in doubt, for without it, the Task Force would have been badly mauled, and the ground forces, had they got ashore,

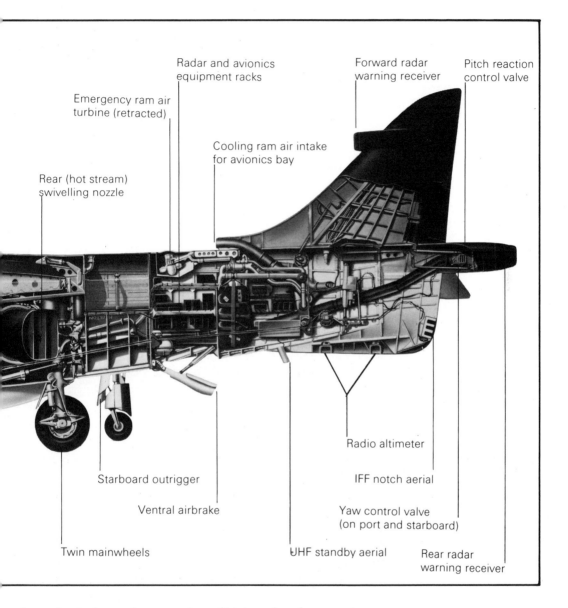

Radar and avionics equipment racks

Forward radar warning receiver

Pitch reaction control valve

Emergency ram air turbine (retracted)

Cooling ram air intake for avionics bay

Rear (hot stream) swivelling nozzle

Starboard outrigger

Ventral airbrake

Twin mainwheels

Radio altimeter

IFF notch aerial

Yaw control valve (on port and starboard)

UHF standby aerial

Rear radar warning receiver

brought the lesson home to the politicians that they require more flexibility in their naval air equation.

The success stories of the air war are obvious—the Harrier and Sea Harrier have more than proved their capabilities; as have the helicopters in all their guises. Anti-ship missiles launched from even more so. However, the operation could not have been carried out by air power alone. The lesson of inter-service co-operation has been proved in action once more. It has certainly aircraft are taken as a much more serious threat than perhaps was believed hitherto; while most of the SAMs used have also been shown to be effective, notably the Seawolf and Rapier. The success of the Sidewinder AAM has also been a boost for the planners, as BAeD have a more effective and cheaper successor on the drawing boards.

Tactically, the air forces have re-learned that even in this day of missiles, a curtain of lead thrown up by light anti-aircraft guns and even small arms can still down an aircraft. The need for stand-off airfield attack weapons has not gone unrecognized. However, more than anything else, the calibre and courage of the aircrews and their supporting personnel has been proved beyond doubt. When called upon to do their job, be it fly a Sea Harrier or service a dunking sonar, they have got on with the task in the face of adverse conditions and apparently overwhelming odds.

Disagreements between commanders

There have been reports of disagreements between the Task Force Commander and the Land Forces Commander. Admiral Woodward may have wanted to make a rapid direct assault on Port Stanley early in May, and may have been talked out of it by General Moore, but it is unlikely that either commander would have confided in TV and newspaper reporters. Differences between land and sea commanders are nothing new, despite what some reporters thought.

More alarming were reports that the troops ashore complained of 'Windy Woodward' and his reluctance to station his two carriers closer to the San Carlos beachhead. It was even suggested that the Admiral stayed so far east that he could qualify for the Burma Star. Sadly this is a reflection on the inexperience of the journalists who reported this 'bivouac gossip' at face value. Even if there was friction at high level, junior officers and NCOs are not privy to such deliberations, and their opinions on just why and when certain key decisions are made have little connection with the truth. Anyone who reads history no further back than the Second World War must be aware how little the 'man on the ground' really knows about strategic decisions, and how easily rumours gain credence.

One thing should be borne in mind by critics of the naval tactics: if either of the two carriers had been sunk or seriously damaged the political repercussions would almost certainly have forced the British Government to abandon the operation. Even

A rare photograph of the *Canberra* and supporting frigate in San Carlos Water.

more to the point, if both the *Hermes* and the *Invincible* had been put out of action it would have been General Moore's men who were repatriated in Argentine ships, and the disgrace would have been his, rather than General Menendez'.

Looked at from both angles, the safety of the carriers was paramount, and there could be no military argument for putting them close to San Carlos merely to bolster Army morale. Classic carrier tactics call for the carriers to give themselves plenty of sea room, rather than tie themselves to the invasion area, where they are no more effective and are merely another priority target which needs defending.

One of the more controversial decisions of the campaign was to station the troopship *Canberra* in San Carlos Water. Some naval officers wanted her kept, like the *QE2*, well away from the beachhead, but others on the Staff wanted her close to speed up the build-up of troops. In the event a compromise was reached, and the *Canberra* was moored in a steep-sided bay and withdrawn during the day. Although she was theoretically a sitting duck the cliffs on either side made it impossible for the Argentine pilots to get a clear view of her, and although some near-misses shook her up she was never hit. Incidentally, one of the reasons for choosing

San Carlos was to gain protection from the cliffs against Exocet attacks.

Throughout the campaign there was clear evidence to show that very few people had experience of real warfare. Newspapers and TV talked of 'bloody conflict' when in fact losses were remarkably light, both on land and at sea. Nobody who is well versed in the history of amphibious warfare would regard the loss of two frigates and one large transport as an unacceptable ratio of losses. It has always been a maxim of amphibious warfare that the warships are there to protect the troops, and to lose two frigates in exchange for getting the troops ashore without the loss of a single man was a light price to pay.

Again, memories of Second World War losses should have reminded commentators that small, unarmoured warships *are* easily sunk by bombs. The Argentine Skyhawks were probably dropping 500-lb bombs, twice the weight of the standard bomb used by the RAF against battleships for the first two years of the Second World War.

The landing at Bluff Cove was almost certainly the only bad miscalculation of the amphibious operations, for in retrospect it does not seem to have been an operation worth the risk. On the first day the LSL *Sir Tristram* had landed a lot of ammunition as well as key personnel, securing the position, but when her sister *Sir Galahad* arrived next day she apparently lay in the cove for six hours before beginning to disembark her troops. If it had worked it would have been hailed as a brilliant piece of opportunism, but with hindsight we are entitled to ask if such a success would have advanced the surrender of the Port Stanley garrison.

Perhaps we should be more grateful that there were no more such disasters. Although the fact that Britain won should not cloud the vital deficiencies in her equipment the Falklands Campaign demonstrated the validity of the SAS motto: 'Who Dares Wins'. War is a matter of risk-taking and victory goes to the side which makes fewest mistakes. The whole Falklands operation was a gamble and Britain won the naval and air war mainly because of the following reasons; the almost total absence of the Argentine Fleet; the comparative inexperience of Argentine pilots and the fact that they were operating at the end of their range; a combination of good generalship and luck; the good performance of British aircraft and some of the ships' systems; and most importantly the very high standard of training and morale of British servicemen.

Chapter 7
Conclusion

T he big troopships have come home, the damaged warships have limped in, and a large part of the force got together to liberate the Falklands has returned to its normal duties. But for the Falkland Islanders, the British armed forces and the British nation nothing can be quite the same again.

Although Argentina has refused to admit defeat the words '*de facto* ceasefire' have been taken by the British Government to mean that no more military operations will be mounted against the islands. However the claim to the islands has not been dropped, and the British are left with a major headache of what to do for the future.

Clearly the neglect of the past two decades will have to be undone, and the first priority for the garrison must be to provide a new military airfield. This means an airstrip at least 8000 ft long, capable of taking the largest military and commercial aircraft.

It is now recognized that the most costly mistake made by the British was to rely on the original short airstrip, for it meant that there was never any possibility of stationing significant air forces in the Falklands. This time the threat of Argentine air attack means that at the very least a squadron of Phantom interceptors will be based on Port Stanley, and possibly a squadron of Buccaneer bombers. Provided that adequate ground defences and base facilities are provided as well there is no need for more aircraft to be based there. From Ascension it will be possible to reinforce the islands at short notice.

Estimates of the garrison needed to defend the Falklands

The liner, *Canberra*, the 'Great White Whale' docks at Southampton with an exuberant escort of small craft (*above right*). More than 10 000 people welcomed the *Hermes* back to Portsmouth (*below right*). *Hermes* alone recorded shooting down and damaging 43 Argentine aircraft and final British claims were 109 aircraft destroyed from all causes, including 31 A-4 Skyhawks and 26 Mirages and Daggers.

vary but 3000 men is the generally accepted level, sufficient to deter any further aggression but not too many men to strain the islands' resources. The garrison will, of course, need helicopters to give them the ability to move rapidly around the islands. Another requirement will be adequate anti-aircraft defences, in addition to the RAF interceptors and radar cover.

The Royal Navy will be required to base at least a squadron of four ships on Port Stanley for some time, probably a missile destroyer and three frigates, in addition to the ice-patrol ship *Endurance*. The lack of docking facilities at Port Stanley can be met by providing a repair ship, and more important repairs could be carried out if an agreement is negotiated with Chile to use their ports.

For the moment the garrison is much more concerned with cleaning up after the Argentine occupation and removing the thousands of mines sown indiscriminately around Port Stanley. The problem is exacerbated by the peaty soil, which allows mines to sink in. Parts of the uplands around Port Stanley may never be cleared for that reason, as the mines have already disappeared into the peat. Nor are these the only mines. Two Royal Navy mine countermeasures vessels (MCMVs) have been sent to the Falklands to make sure that Port Stanley harbour has not been sown with magnetic or other influence mines.

For the future the major decisions to be made are political. Are the Falklands to be developed commercially, and is any attempt to be made to seek a reconciliation with Argentina? Merely granting the islanders self-determination under United Nations trusteeship will not remove the threat of military intervention at some future date. On the other hand relations between the Falklanders and the British on one side and the Argentines on the other are too embittered to make any sort of 'lease back' or shared Argentine-British rule possible for another 25 years.

A glimmer of hope lies in the turmoil which followed the British defeat of the Argentine defenders. At one moment the Junta seemed unshakeable, having the backing of a united people, but the realization that most of the Junta's claims had turned out to be false discredited General Galtieri and forced his resignation. Growing disillusionment with all-military rule has given new strength to the calls for a return to some sort of democratic rule, and out of this may come a more stable state of affairs. At the start of the conflict nobody would have predicted that General Galtieri

would be deposed and equally nobody can predict what sort of changes will occur in the next few years.

For the British the Falklands experience means a drastic review of defence policy. Not only must the war be paid for, but the lessons must be learned and the losses must be made good. Early in July it was announced that another 14 Sea Harriers would be bought, 7 replacements and 7 new aircraft, in addition to several helicopters to make good losses. The sale of HMS *Invincible* to Australia has been revoked, for clearly it would be politically impossible to justify immediately after the ship has played such a vital role.

The Naval Staff have made their views known. All three *Invincible* class support carriers should be maintained, four Type 22 frigates should be ordered to replace the *Sheffield, Coventry, Ardent* and *Antelope* (one Type 22 was ordered in July, but this was one previously authorized). In addition the proposed cutback in the surface fleet should be abandoned, and a minimum active strength of 50 destroyers and frigates should be maintained.

The defence debate will continue, and as before it will be about value for money. Although the Defence Secretary's proposed cuts made financial sense they will be hard to justify politically. But whatever is desirable politically, the fact remains that the cost of defence is rising steeply. The threat from sophisticated weapons demands sophisticated defences. A typical comparison of costs would be:

Area defence SAM—£30 million
Long-range sonar—£35 million
Point-defence system—£30 million
ECM equipment, helicopters, etc—£35 million.

Merely increasing the speed of a warship from 25 knots to 29 knots can add enormously to her cost, particularly when plotted in terms of what it would cost to run her over a number of years, the so-called 'through-life cost'.

The dilemma for the British is that a more flexible navy, one that has the ability to move 'out of theatre' to deal with such unforeseen eventualities as the Falklands invasion is going to be much more expensive and more difficult to equip than a single-role navy. There is a political commitment to NATO and Europe to keep 55 000 troops in Germany, and a military need to maintain the offensive and defensive strength of the RAF.

Previous defence reviews have failed to reconcile these contradictory objectives, but the post-Falklands debate may bring some more radical thinking to bear on the problem. One such solution would be to abolish the expensive married quarters in Germany, moving the soldiers' dependants back to Britain and merely stationing troops in temporary (ie, front-line accommodation in rotation). This principle comes naturally to the Navy, but has never been tried in peacetime for the Army. Whether it would work or not is arguable, but what is certain is that the provision of shops, schools and married quarters for the British Army of the Rhine adds enormously to the cost of stationing troops in Germany.

Whatever the size of the future Royal Navy and its make-up, the experience of the Falklands will result in changes of equipment. Clearly training will benefit from practical experience, and NATO as a whole will benefit as well. There is likely to be a great deal of interest in anti-missile defence, both in the field of passive countermeasures and in point-defence gun- and missile-systems.

The biggest beneficiary of all this is likely to be the Sea Harrier. After many years of development the STOVL aircraft has shown what it can do, and the next step is likely to be a supersonic variant. The US Marine Corps and the RAF already have the AV-8B Harrier II on order, but this is still a subsonic ground-support aircraft. Many navies, particularly the Italian and French, have been looking at the Sea Harrier, and undoubtedly its heroic performance in the Falklands against supersonic aircraft has settled many doubts about its inherent capabilities.

The inquest into the Falklands will go on for some time, which is only right, as it is the first major conflict at sea since 1945. Although we can all read lessons into the events, we should bear in mind that every previous naval conflict has generated more confusion than enlightenment. In most cases the wrong lessons have been learned, and it would be surprising if the Falklands War proved to be any different.

Appendix A
Falklands Chronology

Friday April 2

Argentine land, sea and air forces begin invasion of the Falkland Islands and South Georgia.

British announce formation of Task Force to recover them

Saturday April 3

Royal Marines on the Falklands captured by Argentine special forces and marines. Royal Marines at Grytviken (South Georgia) destroy Alouette and Puma helicopters and damage corvette *Granville* with anti-tank weapons, before surrendering.

Britain breaks off diplomatic relations with Argentina.

Monday April 5

Task Force sails for Falklands led by HMS *Hermes* and HMS *Invincible*; remainder of ships sail later.

Thursday April 8

Britain imposes 200-mile Exclusion Zone around the Falklands to commence April 12.

Tuesday April 13

EEC approves one month's ban on Argentine imports.

Wednesday April 21

Sea Harrier intercepts Boeing 707 with Argentine markings near fleet. Subsequently claimed to have been a military reconnaissance aircraft.

Saturday April 24

Task Force loses Sea King helicopter, ditched.

Sunday April 25

Britain announces Exclusive Air Zone around the Falklands.

British forces recapture South Georgia without casualties, but two Gazelle helicopters lost. Argentine submarine, *Santa Fé*, hit and driven ashore by British helicopters.

Friday April 30

Britain imposes Total Exclusion Zone around the Falklands.

Saturday May 1

RAF Vulcan bombs runway at Port Stanley: later Sea Harriers follow up, and raid Goose Green.

Daggers attack warships bombarding Port Stanley; 1 Dagger shot down by Sea Harriers, 1 shot down by Argentine gunfire. Argentine Canberras attack Task Force; 1 shot down and 1 claimed damaged by Sea Harrier. HMS *Arrow* damaged by splinters.

Sunday May 2

Argentine patrol vessels *Alferez Sobral* and *Comodoro Somellera* fire on Sea King from *Hermes*; *Somellera* sunk and *Sobral* damaged by Sea Skua missiles from two Lynx helicopters.

Argentine cruiser *General Belgrano* sunk by two torpedoes fired from British submarine *Conqueror*; 360 casualties.

Tuesday May 4

British destroyer *Sheffield* hit by AM-39 Exocet missile from Argentine Super Etendards. Ship catches fire; 20 dead.

Sea Harrier shot down while on bombing raid on Falkland Islands; pilot dead. One or more Vulcans bomb runway at Port Stanley.

Thursday May 6

France halts deliveries of Super Etendards to Argentina.

Two Sea Harriers collide in fog; both pilots killed.

Friday May 7

Total Exclusion Zone is extended to 12 miles off Argentine mainland by Britain.

Saturday May 8

20 Sea Harriers and Harriers flown 3500 miles from Yeovilton to Ascension (9 hours).

Argentine Hercules and Mirage escort turned back by Sea Harriers.

Mirage attack on Task Force driven off by Sea Harriers.

Sunday May 9

Another Argentine attempt to fly transports into the Falklands turned back by Sea Harriers.

Sea Harriers attack Port Stanley.
Sea Dart missile shoots down Argentine Puma.
Argentine intelligence-gathering trawler *Narwal*
intercepted inside the Falklands Exclusion Zone; damaged
by two Sea Harriers and boarded from helicopters.

Monday May 10

Sheffield and *Narwal* sink in tow while heading for South
Georgia, as weather deteriorates.

Wednesday May 12

HMS *Brilliant* destroys the two Skyhawks with Seawolf
missiles off Falkland Sound.
Liner *QE2* sails from Southampton.

Friday May 14

British forces raid Pebble Island airstrip.

Sunday May 16

HMS *Alacrity* sinks supply ship *Rio Carcena* at Port King.
Sea Harriers strafe naval transport *Bahia Buen Sucesco* in
Fox Bay.

Tuesday May 18

Fifth Sea King helicopter lost, due to technical fault.

Friday May 21

Sea King helicopter crashes into sea; 21 SAS dead.
1000 troops land at Port San Carlos on East Falkland,
establishing 10-mile bridgehead.
HMS frigate *Ardent* hit by rocket projectiles and sunk;
frigates *Argonaut* and destroyer *Antrim* damaged.

Sunday May 23

Five Argentine Mirages and one Skyhawk reported
destroyed. A further two Skyhawks and one Mirage
claimed to have been destroyed.
Harriers attack three Argentine helicopters. Two claimed
destroyed.
Frigate *Antelope* hit by bombs, one of which fails to explode.

Monday May 24

Antelope destroyed by bomb before explosives expert
succeeds in 'fuzing' it.

Tuesday May 25

Argentina's Independence Day; heavy air battles over
Falklands, during which the destroyer HMS *Coventry* is

sunk by bombs; container ship SS *Atlantic Conveyor* hit by two Exocet missiles, set on fire and abandoned in San Carlos Water; frigate *Broadsword* damaged by bombs.

Thursday May 27

British troops begin to break out of San Carlos bridgehead.

Friday May 28

Capture of Goose Green airstrip and Port Darwin.

Saturday May 29

British troops move east towards Port Stanley
British warships attack positions around Port Stanley.

Monday May 31

British occupy Mount Kent, 12 miles from Port Stanley.
British aircraft attack Port Stanley airfield.
Two Exocet missiles recorded to have been intercepted by British frigates.

Tuesday June 1

Two Harriers shot down while bombing Port Stanley airfield (pilots rescued).
Sea Harriers destroy Argentine C-130 Hercules believed to have parachuted special forces into East Falklands.

Wednesday June 2

Royal Marines capture survivors of Argentine special forces in farmhouse.
Leaflet raids on Port Stanley urging surrender and withdrawal.

Tuesday June 8

Liberian tanker *Hercules* attacked by two unidentified aircraft (after hostilities ended, admitted to be Argentine) and hit by unexploded bomb.
LSLs *Sir Galahad* and *Sir Tristram* severely damaged by air attack in Bluff Cove, with severe casualties; frigate *Plymouth* damaged by bomb; landing craft sunk by bomb in Choisuel Sound.

Friday June 11

QE2 returns to Britain, carrying 700 survivors from sunken ships.

Monday June 14

Argentine troops in Falklands lay down arms; 11 000 prisoners taken.

Appendix B
Those Who Died
Royal Navy and Royal Marine casualties in ships at sea

HMS *Antelope*

Steward Mark R Stephens
Staff Sgt James Prescott (bomb disposal expert provided by 33rd Engineer Regt)

HMS *Ardent*

AB(S) Derek D Armstrong
Lt Cdr Richard W Banfield
AB(S) Andrew R Barr
POAEM(M) Peter Brouard
Cook Richard J S Dunkerley
Acting Ldg Cook Michael P Foote
MEM(M) Stephen H Ford
Asst Steward Shaun Hanson
AB(S) Sean K Hayward
AB(EW) Stephen Heyes
WEM(R)1 Simon J Lawson
MEM(M)2 Alistair R Leighton
AEMN(M) Allan McAuley
ALS(R) Michael S Mullen
Lt Brian Murphy
LPT Gary T Nelson
Cook John R Roberts
Lt Cdr John M Sephton
ALMEM(M) Stephen J White
A/POWEM(R) Andrew K Palmer
A/LMEM(L) Garry Whitford
MEM(M) Gilbert S Williams

HMS *Argonaut*

AB(R) Ian M Boldy
S(M) Matthew J Stuart

SS *Atlantic Conveyor*
>   RN Personnel:
>   AEM(R) Adrian J Anslow
>   CPO Wtr Edmond K Flanagan
>   L/AEM(L) Donald L Pryce
>
>   RFA Personnel:
>   Ch Radio Officer Ronald Hoole
>   Ng Pu
>   Chan Chi Shing

HMS *Coventry*
>   MEM(M) Frank Armes
>   A/CWEA John Caddy
>   MEA(M)1 Paul Callus
>   A/POCA Stephen Dawson
>   AWEM(R)1 John Dobson
>   PO(S) Michael Fowler
>   WEM(O) Ian Hall
>   Lt Rodney Heath
>   AWEMN1 David Ozbirn
>   Lt Cdr Glen Robinson-Moltke
>   LRO Bernard Still
>   MEA2 Geoffrey Stockwell
>   AWEA1 David Strickland
>   AB(EW) Adrian Sunderland
>   MEM(M)2 Stephen Tonkin
>   Asst Cook Ian Turnbull
>   AWEA2 Philip White
>   WEA Ian Williams
>   Kyo Ben Kwo (laundry staff)

HMS *Fearless* **(LCU)**
>   MEA(P) Alexander James
>   A/LMEM(M) David Miller
>   Marine Robert Griffin
>   Clr Sgt Brian Johnston
>   Sgt Ronald Rotheram
>   Marine Anthony Rundle

HMS *Glamorgan*
>   POAEM(E) Michael Adcock
>   Cook Brian Easton

ACAEM David Lee
AEA(M)2 Kelvin McCallum
Cook Brian Malcolm
Ldg Cook Mark Sambles
Ldg Cook Anthony Sillence
Steward John Stroud
Lt David Tinker
POACMN Colin Vickers

Missing, presumed dead:
AEM(M)1 Mark Henderson
AEM(R)1 Brian Hinge
MEM(M)2 Terence Perkins

HMS *Hermes*

Lt Cdr Gordon W J Batt
POACMN K S Casey

Air Group:
Lt Cdr J E Eyton-Jones
Lt W A Curtis
Lt N Taylor

HMS *Invincible*

NA(AH)1 Brian Marsden

HMS *Sheffield*

Lt Cdr David Balfour
POMEM(M) David Briggs
CA Darryl Cope
WEA1 Anthony Eggington
Sub Lt Richard Emly
PO Cook Robert Fagan
Cook Neil Goodall
Lai Chi Keung (civilian laundryman)
LMEM(M) Allan Knowles
Ldg Cook Tony Marshall
POWEMM(R) Anthony Norman
Cook David Osborne
WEA1 Kevin Sullivan
Cook Andrew Swallow
A/CWEMN Michael Till
WEMN2 Barry Wallis

Ldg Cook Adrian Wellstead
MAA Brian Welsh
Cook Kevin Williams
Lt Cdr John Woodhead

RFA *Sir Galahad*

RFA Personnel:
Third Engr Christopher Hailwood
Second Engr Paul Henry
Elect Fitter Leung Chau Dis
Third Engr Andrew Morris
Butcher Sang Yuk Fai Dis

RFA *Sir Tristram*

RFA Personnel:
Bo'sun Yu Sik Chee
AB Yung Shui Kam

Royal Marines★
Mne Paul David Callan
Mne Colin Davison
Sgt Roger Enefer
Sgt Andrew P Evans
Cpl Kenneth Evans
Cpl Peter Ronald Fitton
Lt Kenneth D Francis
L/Cpl Brett P Giffin
A/Sgt Ian N Hunt
Sgt Robert A Leeming
Cpl Michael D Love
Mne Stephen G McAndrews
L/Cpl Peter B McKay
Mne Gordon Cameron McPherson
Mne John Nowak
Lt Richard James Nunn
Mne Keith Phillips
Cpl Jeremy Smith
Cpl Ian Frank Spencer
Cpl Andrew B Uren
Cpl Laurence G Watts
Mne David Wilson

★This list does not include Royal Marines who may have been killed ashore.

Appendix C

Merchant Ships Commandeered for the Task Force

Queen Elizabeth II
67 107 GRT; 963 ft long
Passenger liner requisitioned from Cunard
and equipped with three helicopter pads,
satellite communications etc

Uganda
16 097 GRT; 539 ft long
Educational cruise ship requisitioned from
P&O Cruises and converted to a 1000-bed
hospital ship; converted at Gibraltar early in
April with helicopter deck etc

Norland
12 990 GRT; 502 ft long
Passenger/cargo ferry requisitioned from
P&O Ferries. She was fitted with a
helicopter pad between the bridge and
funnel, and carried 1000 troops

Europic Ferry
4190 GRT: 451 ft long
Passenger/Ro-Ro cargo ferry requisitioned
from European Ferries

Geestport
7730 GRT; 521 ft long
Passenger/cargo ship chartered from the
Geest Line. She was fitted with satellite
communications and a helicopter deck,
and was one of the most useful
acquisitions, with good speed.

Contender Bezant
11 445 GRT; 567 ft long
Ro-Ro cargo ship chartered from Sea
Containers

Elk
5463 GRT; 495 ft long
Ro-Ro cargo ship requisitioned from P&O
Ferries. She was armed with 2 40-mm
Bofors guns, a helicopter deck and three
Sea King helicopters

Canberra
44 807 GRT; 818 ft long
Passenger liner requisitioned as a
troopship; given two helicopter decks,
Refuelling at Sea (RAS) gear, satellite
communications links and expanded
hospital facilities

Rangatira
8990 GRT; 426 ft long
Ro-Ro ferry requisitioned from Union
Steam Line at the end of May. She left at
the beginning of June carrying 1000
troops, and engineers to repair airstrips

St Edmund
8990 GRT; 695 ft long
Ro-Ro ferry requisitioned from Sealink

St Helena
3150 GRT; 329 ft long
Passenger/cargo carrier requisitioned
from Curnow Stirling, converted to a
minesweeper support ship

Atlantic Causeway Atlantic Conveyor
14 946 GRT; 695 ft long
Ro-Ro cargo/container ships chartered
from Cunard. Both ships were adapted to
operate aircraft, *Causeway* carrying ASW
Sea Kings while *Conveyor* carried RAF
Harriers and Chinooks

Tor Caledonia
5056 GRT; 534 ft long
Ro-Ro ferry requisitioned from
DENMAC/Triport Ferries on May 18 to
carry heavy engineering equipment; set sail
two days later

Baltic Ferry Nordic Ferry
6455 GRT; 495 ft long
Chartered from European Ferries

Merchant Ships Commandeered for the Task Force

Saxonia
12 029 GRT; 575 ft long
Chartered from Cunard

Lycaon Laertes
11 804 GRT; 533 ft long
General cargo carriers chartered from
Ocean Transport & Trading

Scottish Eagle Alvega
33 000 dwt (Alvega 33 329); 689 ft long
Scottish Eagle chartered from Cayzer Irvine
and *Alvega* from the Silver Line.

Balder London
19 980 dwt; 560 ft long
Tanker chartered from Ugland UK

Cordella Farnella
1210 GRT (Cordella 1240); 230 ft long
The above four deep water stern trawlers
were requisitioned from J Marr & Sons for
conversion to Extra Deep Armed Team
Sweepers (EDATS), to sweep influence mines.

Junella
1615 GRT; 217 ft long
Equipment from RNR sweepers was used to
equip two of them, and with the **Pict** (below)
they were the only requisitioned ships whose
civilian crews were entirely replaced by RN

Iris
3873 GRT; 310 ft long
Cable ship chartered from British Telecom
and used as a 'despatch vessel' to move
stores from ship to ship

Wimpey Seahorse
1599 GRT; 226 ft long
Oilfield supply vessel requisitioned from
Wimpey Marine

Stena Seaspread Stena Inspector
6000 GRT; 367 ft long
Multi-purpose oilfield support ships
requisitioned from Stena Atlantic Lines.
Seaspread taken up in May as a repair ship
but *Inspector* acquired in June for salvage
work (converted in USA), presumably to
recover important equipment from ships
sunk in Falkland Sound.

**British Avon British Dart British Esk British Tamar
British Tay British Test British Trent British Wye**
20 000-26 000 dwt; 562 ft long
Tankers chartered from BP to freight fuel to Ascension, where it was transhipped to
RFA replenishment ships and storage tanks ashore

Anco Charger
25 300 dwt; 541 ft long
Chemical tanker chartered from Canadian
Panocean-Anco

Fort Toronto
31 745 dwt; 556 ft long
Tanker chartered from Canadian Pacific to
carry water to Ascension

Northella
1615 GRT; 217 ft long
personnel. All five cleared two minefields in
Port Stanley after the surrender.

Pict
1478 GRT; 230 ft long
Deep water trawler requisitioned from British
United Trawlers for conversion to EDATS
minesweeper support ship

Yorkshireman Irishman
686 GRT; 138 ft long
Ocean tugs with 70 tons' bollard pull,
requisitioned from United Towing

Salvageman
1598 GRT; 226 ft long
Ocean tug with 170 tons' bollard pull,
requisitioned from United Towing

British Enterprise III
1595 GRT; 250 ft long
North Sea diving support ship, chartered
from BUE Ships

Merchant Ships Commandeered for the Task Force

In addition to the above ships the following merchant ships were taken over for Falklands duties:

Astronomer 27 867 GRT container ship, requisitioned from T & J Harrison late in June; took RAF Harriers and spares to Port Stanley

Avelona Star Motor ship chartered from Blue Star Line; fitted with helicopter deck; departed June 10

Cedarbank Tweendecker chartered from Bank Line

Corona Cortina Swedish chemical tankers chartered to freight chemical cargoes to Ascension, and then returned to owners

Eburna 19 763 dwt tanker chartered from Shell

Esso Fawley 11 064 dwt chartered tanker but then quickly returned

Finnanger 37 797 chartered Norwegian tanker but quickly returned

Luminetta 24 951 dwt tanker chartered from Cunard on April 20, but returned two days later

Orionman 6176 dwt tanker chartered from Rowbotham Tankships but quickly returned

Strathewe Tweendeck heavy lift ship chartered from P&O; left June 28 carrying Army landing craft *Antwerp* and *Arromanches*

Vinga Polaris 8000 dwt tanker chartered from Vinga Tankers but quickly returned

G A Walker 30 607 dwt tanker chartered from Pacific but quickly returned

Some chartered ships were returned to their owners shortly afterwards as they were found to unsuited to naval use (either because of inadequate communications or incompatible cargo-handling equipment). The final total was 56 merchant ships, many of which merely carried equipment from the United Kingdom to Ascension. Most of the requisitioned ships, however, served in the War Zone with the Task Force.

Picture Credits

Black and white

API page *125*
Aérospatiale page *69*
BBC TV News page *119*
Frank Spooner via *Defence* page *131*
FMA via *Defence* page *33*
Michael Lennon page *116*
MoD pages *23, 36, 40, 45, 73, 82*
Plessey Radar page *113*
Press Association pages *26, 46, 49, 52, 55, 56, 60, 64, 66, 74, 77, 81, 84, 88,*
 90, 93, 95, 99

Colour

Section 1 (pages 32-33)

British Aerospace page *1*
BBC TV News pages *4, 5, 6, 7*
Press Association pages *2, 3, 8* (top)
Westland Helicopters page *8* (bottom)

Section 2 (pages 96-97)

BBC TV News pages *1, 2, 3, 4, 6-7* (top and bottom left), *8*
Press Association pages *5, 7* (bottom right)